# MOSH (MOBILE SHELL): A New Remote Access

## Remote Access

## By Aditya Raj

# PUBLISHED BY

Amazon

This book is inspired by the work of Keith Winstein who has written the Mosh protocol along with Anders Kaseorg, Quentin Smith, Richard Tibbetts and Keegan McAllister.

# Preface

"MOSH (MOBILE SHELL): A New Era of Remote Access" is based on author's learning at University of Bedfordshire, Luton, United Kingdom. It precisely elaborates selected areas and topics from remote access, its protocols and a new protocol (Mosh) for remote access and does not follow the style and format of a text book. Readers are expected to be quite familiar with the fundamentals of Computer Networking. This book helps to understand the configuration and implementation of Mosh in a network for remote access instead of SSH. Some topics which are discussed in this book are not strictly under the networking domains. Moreover, some supported services such as DHCP, DNS and SSH have also been discussed and implemented in this book. Mainly, this book concentrates on the needs of a new protocol for remote access which can replace the SSH and fills all its flaws.

Aditya Raj

adityaraj_sharma@ymail.com

# Abstract

In the contemporary time, internet is the main mode of communication in daily life even though we all know the truth that it is the most unreliable and unsecured approach. Nevertheless, there is no other alternative of this approach. Here the significant of SSH materializes in the market with a protected ambience for the diffusion of data and files. It is the most preferred, acknowledged and immune course of action for the communication applications. It accommodates the remote access to the server with high security for the users. The level of remote access has ameliorated to the next level through SSH as it secures the data transfer by offering the protected tunnel. Other applications such as SFTP and SCP also utilize SSH channel for its secure functionality.

Even though, the secure remote login is possible through SSH and it has become the sine qua non part in all industries for protected communication, it cannot eschew itself from some shortcomings. A single TCP connection is used during the SSH connection which embed lack of roaming facility in it. Secondly, it accepts input on "character-at-a-time" mode that enhances delay time (RTT) in today's 3G or 4G network. These limitations are the main cause which leads this book to introduce a novice protocol Mosh (Mobile Shell) that can subjugate these flaws and provide a fast, reliable and robust network connection for remote access.

Mosh can be considered as a more significant and useful component for the mobile users, comparing to SSH. The reasons are as follows. First of all, Mosh is able to maintain continuous session on a frequently disconnecting and changing IP address. Secondly, as the Mosh clients can predict and display the user keystrokes without taking help from the server, Mosh ameliorates the quality of the session in a challenging network.

This book has tried to cover all aspects of remote login, its protocols and the new protocol Mosh.

# Acknowledgement

I would like to convey my ardent admiration and gratitude to my book supervisor **Dr. Dayou Li**, book coordinator **Dr. Simant Prakoonwit** and PG program administrator **Dr. Edita Markute** for their immense help, support and inspiration for my book both professionally and personally. Without their supervision and assistance, completing this book would not have been achievable.

I am also very obliged for the continuous assistance which I received from my family and friends especially **Mrs. Ramyani Das** during this vigorous period.

# Dedication

I would like to contribute this book to my parents and my supervisor **Dr. Dayou Li** for their enormous support towards me and my book. I really feel honored for their unconditional inspiration and assistance for enlighten me to the correct path.

# TABLE OF CONTENT

# Chapter 1

# Introduction

## Objectives :

This chapter contains following:

- A brief glance of the role of remote access in networking.

- Problem statement.

- Impact of this book.

- Concise overview of whole book.

- Aim and objectives of this book.

- Beneficiaries of this study.

It is the quintessential world for those who have massive interest in the concept of remote login and the protocols and the techniques are used for it. These days, organizations are having travel happy cultures which include the working of the employees from their homes, sub branches, remote offices and even a network administrator prefers to maintain users system from his workplace. Moreover, remote access has also convinced medical sector by providing flexibility in nursing and clinical reasoning. In addition, education sector is also utilizing remote access for several learning activities as well as for teaching. Thus, remote access plays a significant role in today's network system. (Hallberg, B. A., 2010)

The needs and requirements of a computer network and data communication are metamorphosing day by day. According to this expansion, complications of the network administration is also enhancing in the same proportion. A network administrator fixes the problems either by physical visit or through remote access into the network. (Kasacavage, V. (ed.), 2003)

There are numerous ways to login into a network remotely. SSH (Secure Shell) is the one of the most famous and effective protocol for remote access which supports various application and functionality. Generally, it helps to maintain applications of web, servers and network devices remotely. SSH offers better and improved security over other remote access protocols like TELNET and Rlogin. However, it could not put aside itself from some flaws in its functionality. Several researches have been also carried out even though remote access through SSH is silently facing some challenges in terms of losing connection while roaming or changing IPs. There are some more limitations from which SSH session suffers during remote access connection. (Forouzan, B.A., 2010)

Mosh- A new application which supports mobile shell technique, can eliminate the regular issues of SSH session, capable of providing the roaming facility, is the central element of this book. This fresh application is based on a new protocol called SSP (State Synchronization Protocol). This protocol has a unique feature of synchronizing server and the client even if the IP address metamorphosis frequently. With the help of SSP, Mosh is able to synchronize "character-cell" terminal emulator. (Hacker News, 2012)

# 1.1: Problem statement

Generally, there are several ways to manage the secure remote login to the server. Among them SSH is the most admired and magnificent application, however, it is based on TCP connection which causes some provoking complication for the users. It suffers with high latency even the payload is small (Single Character) over the network and switching of IP subnets or roaming of the user is not feasible through SSH.

SSH cannot accommodates itself with dicey Wi-Fi, coming from home office to coffee shop (or vice versa) and just employing laptops or the systems to the sleep mode for some time, SSH lost the connection and need to establish again. Moreover, SSH can lead the user to the world of pandemonium if the connection of WLAN is a fragile connection rather than constant because it metamorphosis IP address of the link or collapsing the network quite often. Furthermore, SSH connection produces a high rate of latency over a sluggish connection especially for the mobile users.

This mobile user requires a unique protocol that can maintain the session even the IP address is changing (user is roaming among the different networks) and can reduce the latency even the link is slow. The name of this unique protocol is Mosh which has thoroughly elucidated and implemented in this book.

# 1.2: Concise overview of entire book

This book ushers Mosh, an alternative of SSH in order to eradicate its flaws and assist the users to use Mosh for remote login. The entire book has devoted to obtain the solution of the following questions:

- Why are there some problems in SSH with respect to roaming and latency?
- How does Mosh eliminate these shortcomings of SSH?
- How Mosh has implemented with respect to support roaming facility to the user?
- Are all problems mentioned in the problem statement addressed?

Here the artefact is the implementation of Mosh in such a way that it indulges all those features which the existing system of remote access means SSH has missed. It is the first time when a protocol has implemented in the network to provide switching facility to the users to roam or change their IP addresses and at the same time maintain the previous session without losing even the single line on the terminal emulator.

## 1.3: Book Impact

The main ground of this book is to provide a new technique for the remote login in the world of networking. As maintaining a continuous session over the fluctuating network connection, has always an issue for the network administrators which can be solved through study of this book. The working of this protocol can be influenced the mobile users to adopt the Mosh instead of SSH which really supports roaming without session break even the network is being changed by the users.

A comparative study has made between this mobile technique and other existing technique of the mobile application to incorporate those oversight features which are not the part of existing mobile applications.

## 1.4: Aim & Artefact

The major aim is to create a network which can abrogate the flaws of SSH and implement a new mobile shell technology called Mosh, which almost has the same functionality like SSH but provides few additional functionality like roaming (IP changing is possible during the connection), faster line editing and echoing facility from the client side so that issues like session termination during the intermittent connection, IP roaming (while the previous or existing session discontinue automatically) can be avoided. If adopted practically, this work also aims to assist a network administrator on handling the network server remotely through Mosh instead of SSH. (Referred-interim report)

## 1.5: Objectives

- The main objective is to fill the flaws of the SSH remote login by using MOSH protocol in a network.

- Another objective is to provide the depth understanding of the remote login methods in the network.

- To show the working of MOSH successfully, an experiment will take place by configuring the MOSH server and client, and establishing the connection between them.

- A comparison between functionality of SSH and MOSH would be done which will help to understand the difference between these two terminal emulator remote access protocols. (Referred-interim report)

## 1.6: Persons benefited

This book can be benefited to those network engineers who are new in the world of networking for remote access. They can imbibe massive information not only regarding configuration of Mosh, also about SSH. They can also follow this book to configure DHCP and DNS server as it is the basic work of a network engineer. Moreover, network administrators can also replace the functionality of SSH with Mosh and can offer a better technique to remote users as well as mobile users.

## Summary

This chapter firstly tried to make familiar the users with need of remote access, its protocols and a new protocol Mosh for it. Then problem of existing technology during the remote login has highlighted. The Aim and Objectives have mentioned along with impact and beneficiaries of this study.

# Chapter 2

# Background

## Objectives:

This chapter covers following objectives:

- Brief on remote access.
- Users of remote access services.
- Role of remote access in the organizations.
- Requirements and benefits of remote access for both employee and employer.
- Protocols that supports remote access facility.

# Introduction

This chapter gives a brief explanation about remote access evolution and the protocols which are used for its working. Thus, it is necessary to understand the entire concept of the remote access. A brief history of remote access, about its users, benefits and protocols evolution is illustrated in this chapter.

## 2.1: Remote Access

In the beginning, remote access was known as dump terminals, modems and low performances workstations. On the contrary, nowadays, high speed workstations, modems, terminals and servers are the part of remote access. Kasacavage, V. (ed.) (2003: 4) says that the ability to establish the connection and to get the access over network resources which are distributed internally in a network is called remote access. In this, usually a workstation contains the tools and software for remote access that helps users to get the authorized access in a network from remote site over a phone, ISDN or broadband line to transfer files, read e-mails, executes applications and most importantly to troubleshoot problems.

## 2.1.1: Who Avails Remote Access Services?

It is very necessary to understand the types of users who access the remote access services. According to the Hallberg, B. A. (2010: 123), there are four main categories for remote access users. They are as follows:

1. **Broad Traveler:** Today's this type of the users are the most significant part for any organization who use LAN in the office and also have to use office LAN when they are outside the office.

2. **Narrow Traveler:** The users who have to visit some limited locations for instant organization distributed centre, branch offices, manufacturing sites and so on. They also need to login into the company's LAN network remotely.

3. **Remote Office User:** Users location is fixed in this category. Users login into the LAN to access emails and applications from a single location. This user deals with the storage

of local files, therefore, does not require any file access except use files for the email system.

4. **Remote Office Group:** It is a remote location comprises with two or more users who use company's LAN for definite services. Although, these users have also their meager local LAN.

## 2.1.2: Why Organizations Require Remote Access?

When the techniques like telecommunication, internet, intranet, extranet, email, voice mail, video conferencing and so on, have appearance in the market then we have commenced to figure out about the new access techniques to access any data from anywhere. (Kasacavage, V. (ed.), 2003)

According to the Kasacavage, V. (ed.), 2003: 5), only to provide remote access services to their employees', organizations are investing a huge amount of money between $ 500, 000 to over $ 1, 000, 000 every year. It does not involve the cost of desktops or laptops; it merely involves the cost of software, hardware, different access lines and server equipments.

Remote access offers many helps to the businesses. It reduces employee's travelling which supports the Clean Air Act. Moreover, it also helps with some other legislation such as the Family Leave Act, during the medical emergencies for employee's family as well as for himself. In this scenario, employee can work even he is not in the office. In addition, network engineers or technicians also need to connect with office network while he is on site, road or somewhere else to take the assignments, order equipments, parts and also to manage bill information. As executives are very busy, they also use remote access connectivity to handle the business even from home or road. (Kasacavage, V. (ed.), 2003)

Remote access is also very economical because organizations do not have to set up additional hardware or software for their branch offices. The system and application problems of branch offices can be fixed and troubleshoot remotely through remote access. Furthermore, small organizations are also lending these facilities from giant companies even sometimes they may use their processors too. (Kasacavage, V. (ed.), 2003)

## 2.1.3: Determining Remote Access Requirements

The requirements of the remote access vary from organization to organization. Sometimes, requirements are same still solution may vary because every organization has amalgamation of different remote users. An organization can use either client/server application or monolithic application for remote access on its requirements. (Hallberg, B. A., 2010)

## 2.1.4: Merits of Remote Access

Remote access makes the business more productive. It is an effective way to cut off the costs in any business by removing additional need of space. Employees can also work from home and they can support the organization even if they are ill, have cold, pains or in any other kind of sickness. (Kasacavage, V. (ed.), 2003)

Remote access can be used by those staffs that need to access corporate LAN immediately from anywhere to support the customers at anytime. Moreover, even technical staffs do not require traveling to every branch offices to troubleshoot the problems. Furthermore, the benefits of remote access can be discussed from the prospective of employees and employer. (Kasacavage, V. (ed.), 2003)

**Employees Benefits**

- Communication time has reduced.
- Personal time with family has increased.
- Semblance of freedom and control.
- Better communication.

**Employer Benefits**

- Provide flexibility in recruitment process.
- Increased productivity.
- Absenteeism has deteriorated.

- Communication has become better and fast.
- The space of the office has diminished.
- They can follow regulatory guidelines like "Clean Air and Environment Regulations."
- The major benefit is that it is very economical.

All these merits of remote access can offer an organization a decisive assistance for its employee as well as ameliorate customers comfort.

## 2.1.5: Nature of Remote Access Protocols

Obviously, remote access provides many benefits to both employer and employee. The protocols that can be used for remote access are three types, depends on its evolution namely TELNET, Rlogin and SSH which have shown in below figure 2.1.

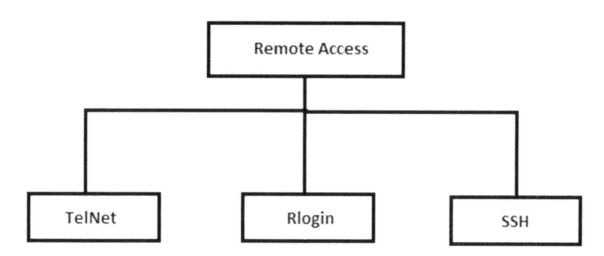

Figure 2.1: Three types of protocol for remote access.

## 2.2: Telnet

TELNET stands for TErminaL NETwork. It is a TCP/IP protocol which is used for providing the virtual terminal to the user for remote access. It was launched by ISO. It makes remote terminal as a local terminal to the users. It is based on client/server application. (Forouzan, B.A., 2010)

There are three main services which are offered by TELNET. First, it provides basic interface to remote workstation through NVT (Network Virtual Terminal). User's systems do not need to understand the concept of remote access, they are compatible to work with these standard interfaces. Second, TELNET uses client and server negotiation mechanism that offers a set of basic options for proper functioning. Lastly, TELNET offers a symmetrical connection to both ends. It means, the client input is neither pressurized by the TELNET to appear from the keyboard nor pressurized client to show output on the display. Thus, it can be said that TELNET uses an arbitrary program to provide client functionality. Moreover, negotiation option can be used by both ends. (Comer, D.E., 2006)

**Security concern of TELNET**

Even though TELNET needs a user name and password to establish the connection between client and server, it suffers from security flaws. A workstation which is attached to a broadcast LAN can get the user name and password very easily with the help of snooper software. Encryption does not play any role in this scenario. (Comer, D.E., 2006)

## 2.3: Rlogin

In the past, Rlogin was used as alternative of TELNET. Rlogin has seeded the idea of "trusted host" which has been used with SSH later. It offers network administrators to select the machines for user's logins and file accessing. It sets balanced login options for all users. The authorizations of remote users are depend on host and user name which offers users to manage their individual accounts. Therefore, it supports users with different name on different machines for instance a user has an account on a machine with name X and on another name Y, still user can login remotely and access his account without using password. It brings the security issues in Rlogin because the only use of IP address or user name cannot be considered as a secure mechanism for user authentication. (Comer, D.E., 2006)

## 2.4: SSH

SSH stands for Secure Shell, which is an effective alternative of TELNET and Rlogin. It has taken control over all limitation of both protocols. SSH associates with TCP to make the connections and provides remote access facility to the users. It offers two new functionalities which TELNET does not support during remote access. First, a secure communication is possible through SSH. Second, SSH allows "independent data transfer" through the same connection which is established for remote access. (Comer, D.E., 2006)

Thus, SSH provides a better and secured service for remote access as compare to TELNET and Rlogin. However, still it has some limitations. These flaws will cover in Chapter 3 literature review and the MOSH (Mobile Shell) protocol will be introduced as a solution of those SSH limitations.

## Summary

Maintaining the remote access services is the most crucial part for the every network administrator as it has become the sine qua nun part of the network in all organizations. These days, remote access is being characterized as the cost effective tool to manage the work from head office to branch offices directly without physical visit. Remote connections can be supported by several ways as various factors need to be considered according organization's requirement. In this chapter, three most prominent protocols TELNET, Rlogin and SSH of remote access has briefly elucidated.

TELNET follows the TCP connection and corroborates the connection between client and server through negotiation process. Rlogin is the next protocol for the same purpose with enhanced technique. However, both protocols encounter security flaws which can be overcome by SSH as it grants an authenticated and confidential remote access. It is developed to support general purpose (multiplexing technique) means other applications can also operate securely through SSH connection; still, it has some limitations which have covered in next chapter with its solution as Mosh.

# Chapter 3

# Literature Review

## Objectives:

Following objectives are covered in this chapter:

- Remote access with SSH.
- Why SSH is not sufficient now.
- Existing technologies which might resolve SSH shortcomings.
- Why need Mosh- a new protocol for remote login.
- Proposed Mosh in a network to replace SSH and its flaws.
- Evaluate Mosh critically.

# Introduction

For remote login and the better administration of the connected computer devices, character cell is the key element which is getting more popular day to day for its features. From the growth of SUPUDUP and TELNET, backing 1970s, the users started getting comfortable with the "text-based" protocols for handling the servers and to get access to the distant resources. (Barrett, D.J. et al., 2005)

## 3.1: SSH (Secure Shell)

In the recent days, SSH is working as a general approach for most of the operating systems which include tablets, smart phones etc. These devices work on a terminal where the fundamental text language has not been changed over the past two decades. (Huang, I.H. et al., 2006)

SSH is the key element for the system administrators through which they can manage the whole network system and its equipments. Not only for the administrators, SSH is equally famous among the developers and the users. Through SSH developers can access and manages the cloud servers and the users get connected with each other through remotely based chat rooms, electronic mails, desktops etc. Nowadays, most of these remote connections arises from the smart phones, laptops etc. These connections are able to maintain through Wi-Fi or other cellular based remote applications which are being provided by SSH. (Forouzan, B.A., 2010; Dwivedi, H., 2004; Zwamborn, D., 2002)

## 3.1.2: Current use of SSH

SSH can be deployed in all types and sizes of the organizations such as retail, transportation, energy & utilities, healthcare, government, educational and financial institution. It assists these industries through various methods such as administrating the security system, providing fast connectivity for the mainframes, giving quick solution for the businesses etc. (SSH, 1995; Forouzan, B.A., 2010)

After providing all these facilities also, is suffering from two main issues which are hampering the effectiveness of SSH. Next section covers these limitations as well as other issues of SSH in detail.

## 3.2: Shortcomings of SSH

First of all, SSH employs only one TCP link and it also does not provide the roaming facility over frequently changing IP addresses, irregular connections between devices etc. As a result, a laptop device is not able to switch from Wi-Fi networks to a single data connection and it is also not able to maintain the connection. Similarly, a smart phone is unable to pass through or change the network due to SSH connection and every time user has to re-login when he goes to a new range of signal to the old one. (Brockmeier, J.Z., 2012; Schonwalder, J. et al 2009)

Second issue with SSH is that SSH performs its tasks using a "character-at-a-time" manner, where all the predictions or echoes are carried by the server (remote host). In the recent days, while working on an EVDO or 3G network, a full latency takes 0.1 second in order to complete a whole trip but a delay takes place when a high number of data requires to be moved. Because of this issue, SSH protocol proves to be ineffective in 3G networks. Even in the "4G LTE" the loaded time is 5,000 to 40,000 ms. Thus, it can be said that over a high latency network path SSH can be disappointed while editing and typing the lines. (Winstein, K. and Balakrishnan, H., 2012)

Furthermore, SSH has some more snag as it is unable to provide latest screen to the client and working of "Control-c" can take forever because SSH uses TCP link which first fills buffers. It will not create the controversy if octet stream will refer as an incorrect layer of abstraction as SSH avoid replying megabytes whenever interruption occurs and also it sends everything instead of only required data because it cannot recognize the actual data. (Schonwalder, J. et al., 2009; Huang, I.H. et al., 2006)

## 3.3: Existing technologies to resolve these issues

There are few technologies which have been currently utilizing to resolve the above mentioned issues. **EIDs, NIMROD, HIP** are few of those technologies through which the network mobility can be managed in an efficient manner. Apart from these, there is one more approach "**TCP Migrate Scheme**" which helps to develop a point-to-point environment to provide the users mobility without affecting the routing. (Nikander, P et al., 2008; Castineyra, I., Chiappa, N. and Steenstrup, M., 1996; Snoeren, A. and Balakrishnan, H., 2000)

Now coming to another issue of SSH such as irregular connection, a **Session Layer** method has already been developed to show that SSH does not fail to work even if the connection is a long enough. To support this connection few changes are needed to the both ends of kernel and at the same time some modifications are also required in the applications. (Snoeren, A.C., Balakrishnan, H. and Kaashoek, M.F., 2001)

# REX: - One more protocol which can work as a substitute of SSH is REX. This protocol has been made using "self-Certifying File System". It supports roaming and irregular connections over TCP by holding remote calls. Sometimes the TCP connection stops automatically, in this case the user tries to make a new connection with the previous hostname (DNS). After the new connection is established, all the unspecified RPCs are being sent from both of the sides which were reserved in cache memory. While activating the roaming facility, REX needs a "TCP timeout" through which automatic roaming to any recently visited address (acknowledged by the server from user) becomes possible (Kaminsky, M. et al., 2004)

# DTLS (Datagram Transport Layer Security): - Sometimes the systems do not seem to use the transport layer security. Instead of that, it uses cryptographic module. Core reason behind this scenario in DTLS if the client does not require any roaming facility this protocol omits that. Also DTLS cannot work without the cache memory and public keys which finally resulted into a complicated implementation procedure. (Kothmayr, T. et al., 2012; Rescorla, E. and Modadugu, N, 2006)

## 3.3.1: Current speculation techniques

**BSD: -** The operating systems which are based on BSD technique employ LINEMODE method for using TELNET where client has to execute the task of line editing and character echoing. However, this line mode technique is not being used nowadays because it fails to work with such programs where "raw" mode is used for the terminal. Some acknowledged libraries such as read line and applications like email reader or text editors use this technique. Till the year 2010 kernel was not able to maintain TELNET LINEMODE and at the same time SSH also could not find any substitute of that. (Borman, D., 1990; Linux Git, 2010)

**SUPDUP:** - It employs another local editing protocol through which a whole text editing can be performed locally and can also be uploaded in batches. Host application is needed for encoding SUPDUP's conjoint functionalities in its own language so that SUPDUP can assist the terminal on how to give response to the user keystrokes, how to select the characters for word wrapping etc. practically EMACS is the only text editor which has implemented "SUPDUP-local editing protocol". (Winstein, K. and Balakrishnan, H., 2012)

## 3.4: Limitations of existing technologies

In the beginning, all above technologies got the popularity and appeared in the market as an effective solution for SSH issues. However, as the use of these methods increased, at the same time the numbers of loopholes were also increasing which lowered their credibility in the market for mobile use. Users using HIP get interrupted connection for real time application because CPU has to do several calculations such as Diffie-Hellman, RSA and DSA but the session Layer approach which can provide the intermittent connection, requires some specific modification to the both end which is a time consuming process for an administrator in his busy schedule. The problem of REX is that it cannot roam automatically. The user has to reconnect with the server or network. The structure of DTLS is very complicated as it needs reply cache, cryptographic keys and also it cannot support roaming. Furthermore, not only those technologies failed which provide the roaming and irregular connection, the current methods on speculation also failed in rectifying the SSH line editing problems. The BSD based editor LINEMODE could not work with all programs especially when the terminal holds on "raw" mode. Another technology regarding speculation is SUPDUP which needs various alterations on host application to work with it. Unfortunately, all these existing technologies are not enough to fulfill the limitations of SSH completely and time has come to resolve these issues of SSH which will be resolved in this book through a new protocol- Mosh.

## 3.5: Need of Mosh (Mobile Shell) to overcome the flaws of current methods

SSH was introduced in 1995 which is a long period of time since then to now. It served the networking world in various ways and still continuing. As everything has its peak time and then it has to face a dark side. The problems of SSH which have mentioned above, tried to rectify through several technologies, however they could not pave the correct road map for SSH. Finally, a new protocol Mosh has introduced and implemented in a network to replace the SSH.

## 3.6: Proposed Mosh protocol

This book has analyzed both the issues and has given a solution for both of the problems including other issues. In one word the solution is Mosh which provides roaming facility over the regularly changing IP addresses, irregular or marginal connections. It can also predict the client's echoes without the server assistance. Not only these, while using the Mosh a remote server acts like local device because user can see the keystrokes instantly on the screen even if he is using a full screen email reader or text editor.

Mosh acquires these characteristics because it performs at a complete diverse layer comparing to SSH. The main difference between SSH and Mosh is, SSH works with a" client side terminal emulator" where as Mosh includes a "server side terminal emulator". As the device's screen status is maintained as a picture by both client and server, it is easy for Mosh to maintain the disconnected network and predict the local editing. (Blewitt, A., 2012; Mosh, 2012)

A server can omit an in between screen status. As a result the device can regulate its interchanging networks, to enhance the link's speed, so that no buffering can take place. However, in case of SSH, a client's old screen status cannot be omitted. SSH requires sending every single data as the aftereffect is unknown. To analyze this situation practically, it can be said that in Mosh, one can use "control-c" to finish a fugitive server-based procedure running in between an RTT. There are two major phases, based on which, Mosh's design has been made. These phases have described in section. (Winstein, K. and Balakrishnan, H., 2012)

# Phase 1: SSP (State Synchronization Protocol)

SSP can be found on acme of UDP (User Datagram Protocol). The main task of SSP is to manage the abstracted objects in the presence of insignificant network, irregular connectivity and roaming facility. There are three modules on which SSP is based. First is cryptographic module that offers authenticity and data or messages gets confidentiality as well. Second is datagram layer to transmit the UDP packets throughout the network. Lastly, transport layer through which the current state of the object can be conveyed to the remote system or host. All impact of these three modules is described below in detail. (Winstein, K. and Balakrishnan, H., 2012)

# Cryptographic Module

AES-128 a symmetric key encryption of the "Offset Cookbook (OCB)" is the key element on which the security of this module is constructed. AES-128 can provide a decent range of authenticity and privacy by a single secret key of 128-bit. There are some specific requirements for OCB which includes that every plaintext needs to be merged with an exclusive 128-bit arbitrary number (Nonce). Apart from this another increasing sequence number of 63-bit and a flag for proper direction required. By using this element a remote user can obtain this guarantee that each packet he sent before was successfully received. However, the theory of idem potency comes into light while managing the repeated and recorded packets by SSP. Every time a remote host receives a datagram it symbolizes an idempotent process on the side of the recipient. The remote site receives instruction from a "diff" on building state "m" when the preceding state was "n<m". The outcome expresses that the need for maintaining a "reply cache" by SSP can be omitted. (Mosh, 2012)

# Datagram Layer

Through this layer an encoded connection can be maintained and reached to the remote user. The datagram layer maintains the encrypted connection to the remote host. After making the connection, transport layer sends obscure payloads to it, and then the next work for the datagram layer is to place those payloads into packets, and then sends the packets to the next layer which is the cryptographic layer and finally sends the ensuing cipher content as a payload of UDP. This layer helps to determine and estimate the timing for each network pathway and it also keeps track record of a client's port number and IP address. (Winstein, K. and Balakrishnan, H., 2012)

**Client roaming:** - An unchanged socket address can be maintained for a lifelong connection through datagram layer. Hence, this server on which the socket address is being maintained does not have the permission to travel but the client can travel and change its public port number and IP address at any time, such as the client can travel from or to NAT. The clients present socket address is generally maintained by datagram layer. Every time the server receives and authenticates datagram from the client with a higher sequence number (which has never been previously received), the server make a provision for the new number and it also stores the address through which the packet has come and declares it as a fresh socket address for that client. (Winstein, K. and Balakrishnan, H., 2012; Mosh, 2012)

The result of this process includes an automatic roaming. The client sometimes does not even come to know that the IP address has been changed. Transport layer takes the responsibility to inform the server of the new IP address of specific client by sending infrequent heartbeats. As packets with greater sequence number (which has never been previously received) are only considered by the server, roaming performance becomes constant for reordering packets and as a result, an attacker does not get any success in sending same old packets received from an old client to the server. (Nosulchik, A., 2012; Mosh, 2012)

# Transport Layer

Through transport layer, recent contents of a "local state" can be synchronized to a remote user and the opposite can also be done. There are mainly two persons involved in the implementation procedure. The sender and the receiver, for each case one of the persons requires to get involved. As example, while working with Mosh, server behaves like the sender for the screen status and the receiver helps in the user contribution. It is vice versa when the client helps in the user contribution as a sender and the receiver helps in the screen states. SSP works as a doubter for the elements received or sent. The objects or elements which are being sent have to be supportive for the "four-function interface". (Nosulchik, A., 2012)

# Phase 2: Speculation

SSP and Mosh both work together to control and coordinate the state of the terminal screen from both client and server side. While doing this, every single time a new upshot takes place with display of a fresh "keystrokes" on the screen and the conjunctively the user requires to take a guess regarding that upshot. After rechecking the user's prediction, screen sometimes needs to get refurbished. (Gauger, M., 2012; Winstein, K. and Balakrishnan, H., 2012)

## A Remote Terminal with Speculative Local Echo

A "terminal emulator" has been employed for supporting this Mosh protocol which follows the State Synchronization Interface. After receiving all the user keystrokes, the server applies those and also maintains the respected reference (belongs to the "terminal state"). At this time, the client also predicts about the effect about the keystrokes which finally affected the terminal and most of the times the users are able to theoretically employ those keystrokes on an instant basis. If the client understands that the prediction is going in the correct manner, he decides that how much confidence he can have in order to display his guesses to the remote users (in this case the guesses need to be crossed 100 ms, so that the user do not get any misconception). However, infrequent mistakes can take place but it need to be deleted under an RTT instantly. (Sudobits Blog 2012; Mosh, 2012)

## 3.7: Critical evaluation

In this section a critical evaluation on Mosh has been made based on the above discussion. Hence, after this detailed research it can be stated that Mosh has made the remote access more flexible by adding facilities like roaming, intermittent connection and fast interactive terminal support which is able to remove all the current flaws of SSH. There are some other technologies like HIP, REX, SUPDUP etc which had already tried to work on the issues of SSH but prove to more effective. This is the only protocol which provides mobility as while Mosh is being used as a protocol in the network, the user does not need to stay at the same place for establishing a new session. IP roaming is possible with this protocol. Not only this, latency has also reduced in Mosh as it does not follow "character-at-a-time" mode which SSH does.

As every coin has two different sides, this new protocol also posses few difficulties. Although, Mosh's effectiveness is not being affected by these difficulties but because of these difficulties, Mosh cannot be called a perfect technique for remote login. There are several facilities which Mosh possess, SSH does not but the main demerit of Mosh is that IPv6 is not supported by Mosh. Nowadays the use of IPv6 is growing rapidly as IPv4 is almost acquired by most of the organizations and supply is limited. Another limitation of this magnificent protocol is that only through UTF-8 character input is feasible in Mosh. It means Mosh cannot deal with all of the input methods; UTF-8 is only preferable for it. However, all these limitations of Mosh are not genuine enough as the source of this information is not completely authenticated despite of adopting a diligent and deep research method. (Nosulchik, A., 2012; Hacker News, 2012)

## Summary

A comprehensive study has reviewed in this chapter as it contains the literature review which is the heart of this entire discussion. SSH has analyzed as the current method for remote access and seemed like quite famous among network administrators to handle the network and server remotely. However, study shown that it has some limitations which obstructing the work of mobile users as well as facing problems over high latency path. A depth research has made to collected the information about existing technologies through which these flaws of SSH could control. Unfortunately, all existing methods failed to fill these issues of SSH which has rectified through a new protocol Mosh. A thorough research has been done against Mosh to know how it removes these limitations and why it can be a better technology rather than all existing methods. At last a critical evaluation has also carried out to know about the dark side of Mosh as well as its benefits for remote login in a network.

# Chapter 4

# Design of the Network

## Objectives:

The following objectives are covered in this chapter:

- Describes scenario and design.

- Essential tools.

- Brief explanation of tools and their implementation.

- Design process.

- Flow charts showing operation methods.

# Introduction

The word design itself evinces the innuendo in the terms of blue print or the portrayal of the book which is based on the paper drawing. Design plays very significant role not merely in networking field, other field such as civil engineering, automobiles etc., it is very crucial. For instance, the construction of any building or bridge does not commence straight way before starting the construction a convincing design is made which visualizes final outcome very clearly. The design of the Mosh protocol has elucidated in this chapter including its functionality in a network for remote access.

## 4.1: Scenario

All basic requirements such as software and hardware are collated in the beginning stages because these are prerequisite which are necessary to comprehend the desired output. The scenario which has taken in this book is how Mosh can be suitable for the remote access in a network instated of SSH which leads the configuration of Mosh's server and client in order to establish a remote connection in a network. In addition, SSH's server and client have also configured to demonstrate the difference between Mosh and SSH's connection.

## 4.2: Required tools

You need to collect all basic requirements such as software and hardware in the beginning stage because these are prerequisite which are necessary to comprehend the desired output. There are several tools which are necessary to design and implement above scenario successfully. These tools are covered as follows in brief.

Note: - You are open to obtain any kind of scenario and required tools which suites you. However, you need client/server architecture.

## 4.2.1: VMware Workstation

The resources of physical hardware map with resources of virtual machine during the installation of VMware software on the system. It provides own CPU, NIC, disks and memory to every virtual machine. There is no need to involve in a lengthy process of rebooting to switch between the different virtual machines. In addition, additional hardware can be also simulated through VMware workstation (VMware, n.d.). Here, it supports more than one operating system (CentOS 5.5) too. Below figure 4.1 confirms this. It is available for all environment such as windows, linux etc.

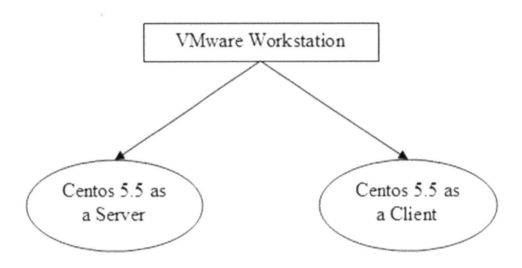

Figure 4.1: VMware workstation install to support more than one Centos 5.5 at same time.

## 4.2.2: Centos

Centos is stand for Community ENTerprise Operating System. It is a freely available Linux of enterprise class for the public with a "Prominent North American Enterprise Linux Vendor". (Centos, 2004)

To implement the scenario server machine (CentOS 5.5) configured to support both server Mosh and SSH as figure 4.2 presents its structure. Furthermore, client machine also configured to offers both client services to the user which has clearly shown through figure 4.3.

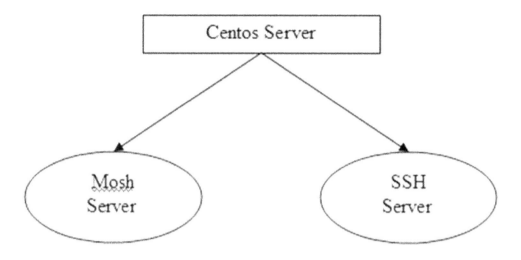

Figure 4.2: Mosh as well as SSH server have configured on same centos.

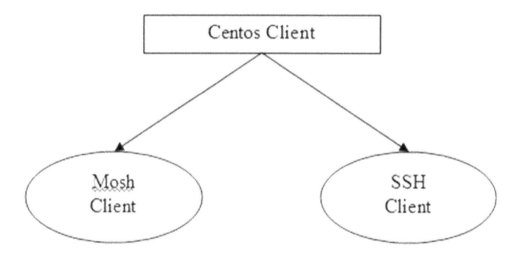

Figure 4.3: On client machine, Mosh and SSH client have configured.

## 4.2.3: Mosh

Mosh has been designed according to our imaginations and assumptions which is based on the user's demand for a mobile application in the network. Furthermore, Mosh provides the client with the most recent screen condition. The security of Mosh is very simplified as it does not have privileged code and users are got authenticated by conventional means. To employ the Mosh, privileged code is not required, it merely ensures that the connection established through single terminal by the use of similar unprivileged user, is how much authenticated and confidential. (Winstein, K. and Balakrishnan, H., 2012)

## 4.2.4: Mosh-Server

It has build to run on the server side and nourishes the application of the remote terminal for the Mosh. It exercises encryption key to secure the connections or sessions and a high port of UDP appends for the session establishment. The range of the UDP port for the Mosh-server is 60000 to 61000 by default. It provides the print facility on "standard output" as well as "detaches from terminal" and a connection is made by the mosh-client, for this connection. It waits till 60 seconds and if the client is not able to associate with it within this time then it exits. Furthermore, Mosh-server also exits from the connection which client terminates the connection. The architecture of mosh-server has been shown in figure 4.5. (Mosh-server, 2012)

SYNOPSIS of the Mosh-Server is "mosh-server new [-s] [-i IP] [-p port] [–c colors] [-command.....]". (Mosh-server, 2012)

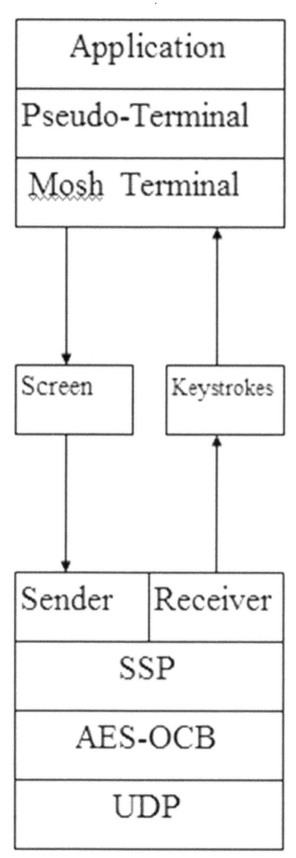

Figure 4.5: Architecture of Mosh server.

## 4.2.5: Mosh-Client

It is a script that is designed to run on client side and set up the connection with the server with the help of mosh-server. It accumulates some required credentials such as port number and IP address of the server and session key to commence the remote communication. For the connections, it lasted for the lifetime. A session key of 22 byte base 64 which is issued from the mosh server, is used with "MOSH_KEY" and this key provides another key of 128 bites AES to secure the confidentiality and integrity of the connection. Mosh-client may be invoked directly to establishing the new session for remote login without the involvement of SSH. The figure 4.6 depicts the structure of Mosh-client. (Mosh-client, 2012)

SYNOPSIS of the Mosh-client is "MOSH_KEY=KEY mosh-client IP PORT" or "mosh-client – c". (Mosh-client, 2012)

The variable of TERM environment gives different colors to the terminal and the option –c is used to figure out the number of those colors.

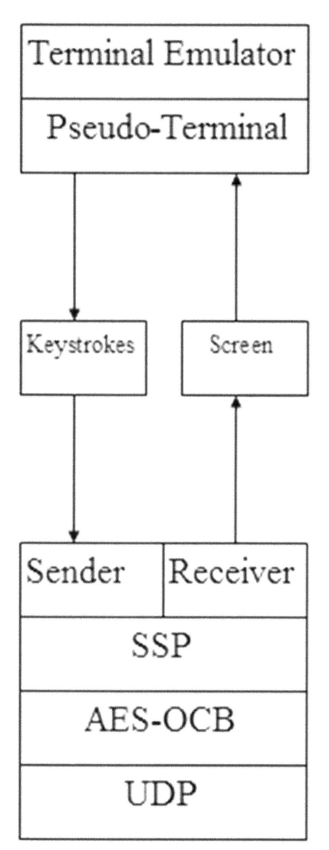

Figure 4.6: Architecture of Mosh client.

## 4.2.6: SSH

The Secure Shell is also based on client-server architecture. It encrypts data transmissions by encryption and a mechanism called RSA is used to authenticate the hosts. It is necessary to explore all authentication methods of SSH before get into the business of configuration of Mosh in the next chapter. There is one more reason to understand about all keys of SSH because Mosh also uses these keys for its connection. In table 4.1 the types of keys, their period, formation and purpose are described briefly and figure 4.8 shows this architecture. (Mann, S. and Mitchell, E.L., 2000)

Table 4.1: - SSH keys with brief description.

| Keys | Formation and Duration | Types of Encryption and Purpose |
|---|---|---|
| Server Keys | It generates with sshd and when it is used first time after that it regenerates each hour. | It is asymmetric RSA encryption which is utilized to authenticate host and disk is never used to store either public server key or private. |
| Host Keys | At the time of compilation, it generates spontaneously and does not regenerate, manually. | The purpose and the type of encryption is just like server key, there is merely only one difference is that disk can be used to store the key. |
| User Keys | User generates it manually and also regenerates if necessary. | It is also RSA asymmetric which is exercised for RSA authentication exclusively. |
| Session Key | It is generated automatically when client chooses a random number during "RSA Host-Based Authentication". It is not possible to generate it manually. SSH session which is symmetric encryption maintained through it. | An encryption tunnel is created which encrypts the transmission of all data between client and server. An algorithm which is also symmetric takes part in this process. |

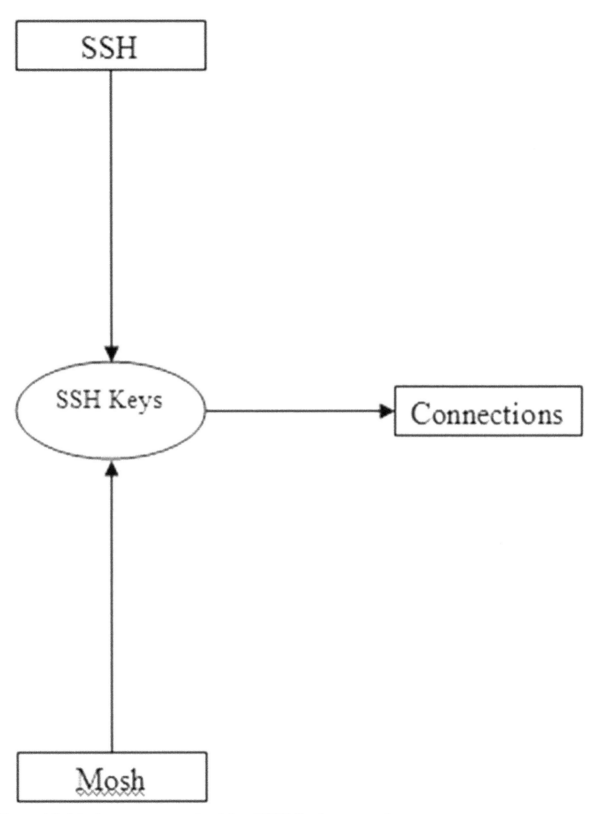

Figure 4.8: Mosh uses same credentials of SSH for the connection.

**Password Authentication: -** In this book, authentication process is based on password authentication for both Mosh as well as SSH as shown in figure 4.9. Client gets into the business with server after authenticating through a password. An adequate user called Rahul has been created on server with the suitable password to demonstrate the scenario. However, above keys are briefly introduced as Mosh uses same credentials of SSH to associate the connection between client and server.

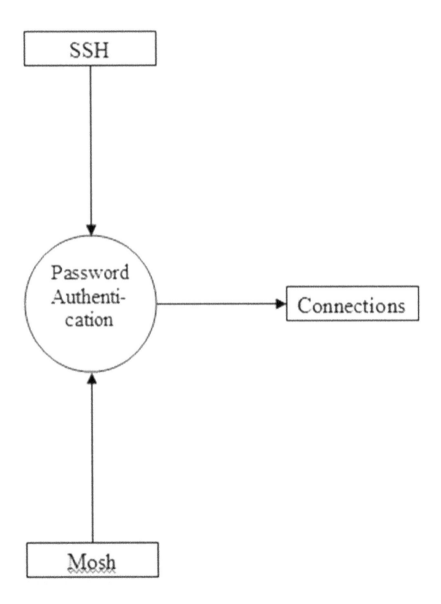

Figure 4.9: This book based on password authentication.

## 4.3: Working design

This section elaborates the working of this book step by step. The working of Mosh has described through the flow diagram 4.10 at the end of this section. The configuration has been discussed in the next chapter. Here, how this whole concept will work for a remote user in a network has enlightened below in details:

- First of all, VMware workstation has installed on the system which has windows 7 as an operating system.

- Two centos 5.5, one for server and another for client have been installed on the same system.

- Both operating systems have configured to work with VMware workstation at a time.

- One of the centos 5.5 has configured as the Mosh server which involved some commands and techniques.

- Server side cannot be configured directly to work as a Mosh server. The configuration of DHCP server also require on the server to lease the IP address to the clients. Now, server has an IP address through which client can make the connection. Furthermore, a DNS server has also configured to work as name resolution. Thus, user does not have to remember the IP address of the server to establish the connection every time.

- Then, other centos 5.5 has configured as a Mosh client which will make connection with Mosh server.

- Now everything is set to establish the connection. Mosh client sends the request to the Mosh server with the user name Rahul. The user Rahul has created at Mosh server which uses password authentication to authenticate the connection.

- If everything will work according to the configuration after the checking of all required credential from the Mosh server then connection will start between client and server.

- However, this book is not only depicting connection between Mosh client and server, it is also working on limitations of SSH connection. Thus, it is necessary to configure the SSH server and client to compare with Mosh connection.

- To compare and propose the new technique with Mosh for remote access, SSH server and client have configured to form another network.

- Then, the connection between SSH client and server has established for the same user.

- To check the functionality between Mosh and SSH, the client has removed from the network (LAN) for some time says 10-20 seconds. When connection has broken then Msoh client makes aware to the user (Rahul) that connection has lost but SSH client does not appear with any information about connection lost which is very painful for a user.

- Again, client has put on the network (LAN) where Mosh client is automatically established the connection with the server from previous connection, however, SSH client could not. User with SSH client has to reconnect to the SSH server from the beginning.

- Thus, user with Mosh client can work without less delay and can commence the work exactly from where he lost the connection. Mosh is able to work even in the intermittent connection, IP changes (Roaming) with less RTT.

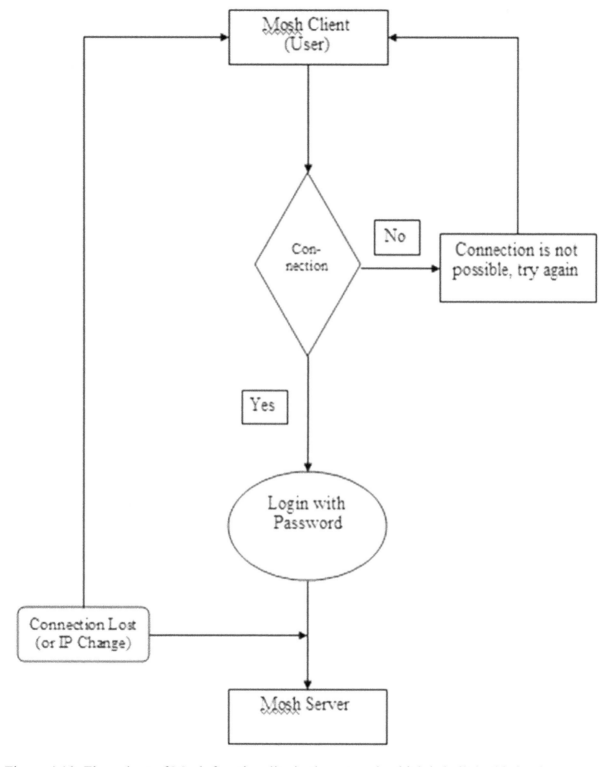

Figure 4.10: Flow chart of Mosh functionality in the network which is built in this book.

## Summary

This chapter has discussed all the required tools which are needed for configuration and implementation of the network. What are these tools and why these are required, was also tried to cover according to their role and purpose in this chapter. The step by step process has been mentioned which brings the imaginary functionality of the Mosh into real. This chapter is provided thorough understanding of the design process.

# Chapter 5

# Network Configuration

## Objectives:

Following objectives are covered in this chapter:

- Provide the information about software requirements.
- Configuration of DHCP.
- Configuration of DNS.
- Configuration of SSH.
- Configuration of Mosh.

# Introduction

This chapter shows and elucidates the configuration of the network which supports Mosh functionality. A proper configuration is the responsible for the efficient working of any network. Thus, this chapter is very crucial as it explains all configurations step by step with all details. Please spend some time here to understand it thoroughly. Directly we cannot configure Mosh before that we have to build up a network.

## 5.1: Software Required

The Mosh has been configured in Linux based environment with the help of virtual machine in this book. For the further and specific details about software see below table 5.1.

Table 5.1: Software required for implementation of the book.

| Software | Description |
|---|---|
| VMware Workstation 9 | It is software which provides the facility to use more than one operating system virtually at the same time. |
| Centos 5.5 | It is a Linux family operating system. It can be used virtually as well as a normal operating system. |

It is not mandatory to use centos as an operating system. Other operating systems such as Ubuntu, Debain, Fedora, Gentoo, Arch Linux, OS X, Android and so on can be also preferred instead of centos. However, this book prefers centos 5.5.

NOTE: - In this book network has created in virtual environment. However, it is not necessary you can implement it in real world scenario.

## 5.2: Configuration Steps

Systematical representation of the required steps has elucidated and the screenshots are referred for better understanding of configuration in below sections.

To perform all these configuration and installation sometimes it is necessary to use internet connection in Centos 5.5. It is quite different procedure to activate internet in VMware and to do it put VMware workstation on bridge or NAT from setting and then go to system → administration → network connection and a new dialog box opens. Here, click on edit option and set dhcp to "automatically obtained IP address settings" then click on probe option to bind the system with MAC/ physical address.

## 5.2.1: Mosh Environment Configuration Steps (Network 1)

**Section 1: -** This section explains the configuration of the DHCP server which would be assigned statically IP address 198.168.0.0/24 on centos 5.5. This task supports the communication between centos server and client. It also elucidates the leasing concept of DHCP server which provides IP address to the client machine.

Both server and client use the DHCP facility to perform many functions over the network. DHCP gives a flexible way to the administrator through "lease" to configure dynamic data or leasable parameters such as domain name system (DNS), IP address net mask, default gateway and so on. A DHCP client request an IP address from DHCP server through broadcasting for their local machine and a DHCP server responses through unicasting. A client has to get back to DHCP server at regular intervals of time to renew its lease. When a client renews its lease then it expires in the course of time and then DHCP server can assign even used lease to other clients.

**STEP 1: Install DHCP mirror file**

- First of all, there is need of DHCP mirror file to start the configuration of DHCP server. The command **"yum install dhcp"** is used to download these mirror files on the server machine which is centos 5.5. Below figure 5.1, shows the working of this command.

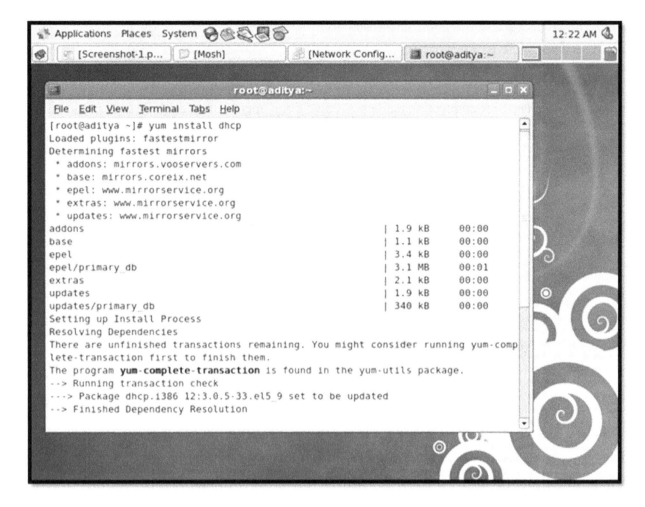

Figure 5.1: Mirror files for DHCP are being installing.

## STEP 2: Configuration of subnet statically

- DHCP server has configured statically in this book on subnet 192.168.0.1/24. Through command **"vi /etc/sysconfig/network – scripts/ifcfg – eth0"** the IPADDR, NETMASK, NETWORK can be configured on which DHCP server will work. See figure 5.2.

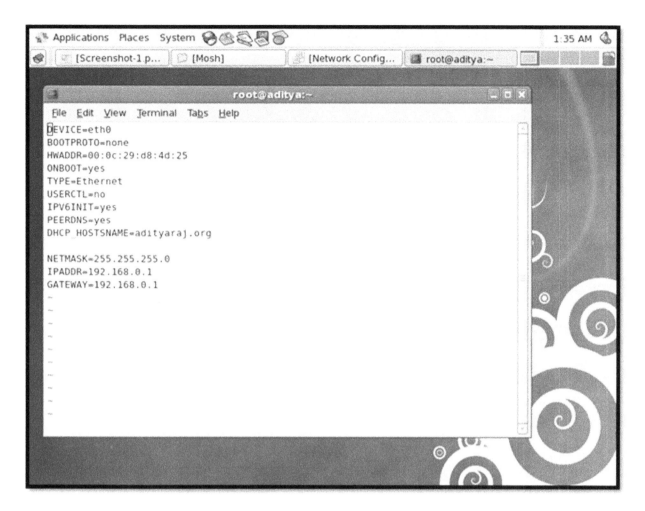

Figure 5.2: Statically altering subnet values.

**STEP 3: Modification in sample file (dhcpd.conf) of DHCP**

- The command **"cp /usr/share/doc/dhcp-3.0.5/dhcp.conf.sample/etc/dhcp.conf"** brings the dhcpd.conf which is a sample file to /etc/dhcpd.conf. it is always safe to work with sample files instead of main file because rectifying the issus in main file can be long lasting process.

- Use command"**gedit /etc/dhcpd.conf** " and set the range of IP address, default gateway and domain name. Figure 5.3, shows this alteration clearly.

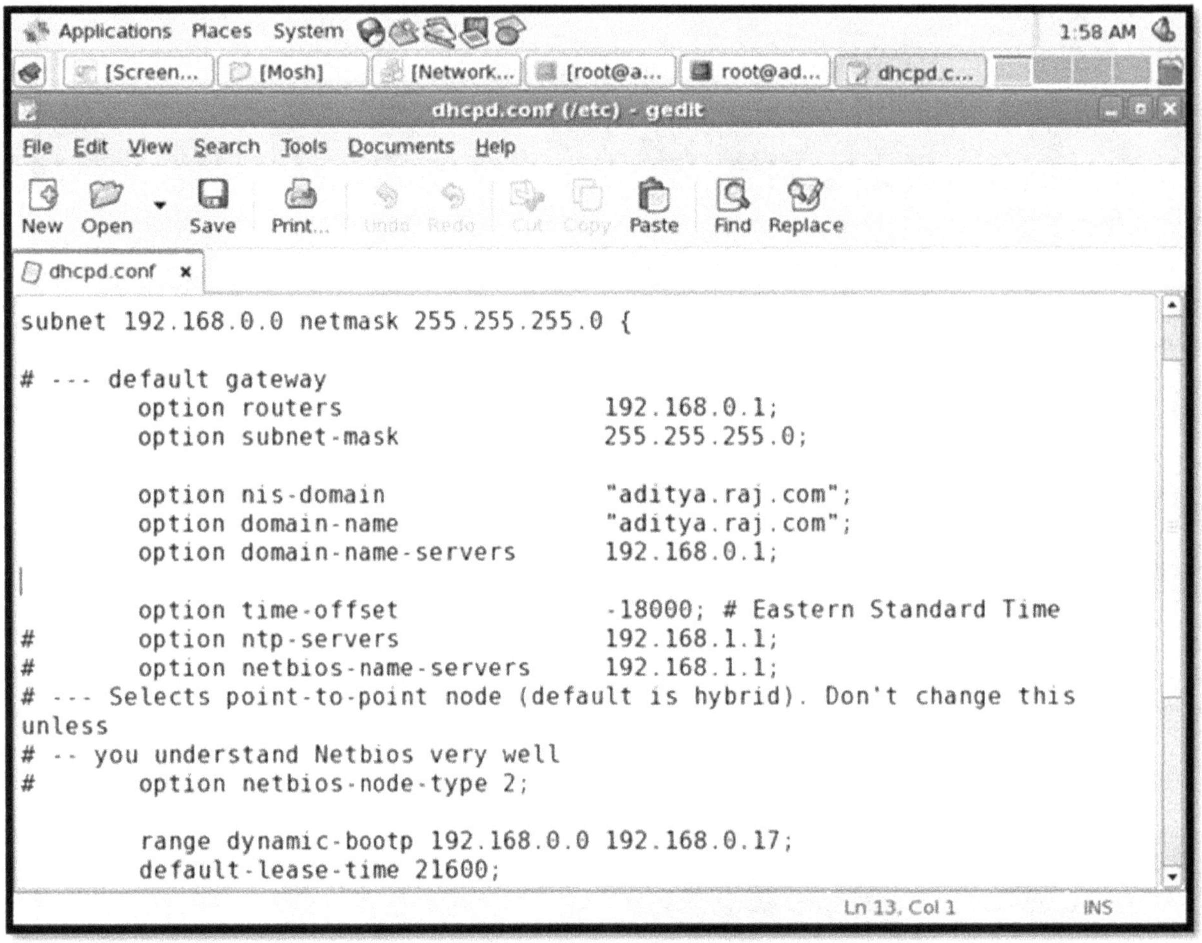

```
subnet 192.168.0.0 netmask 255.255.255.0 {

# --- default gateway
        option routers                  192.168.0.1;
        option subnet-mask              255.255.255.0;

        option nis-domain               "aditya.raj.com";
        option domain-name              "aditya.raj.com";
        option domain-name-servers      192.168.0.1;

        option time-offset              -18000; # Eastern Standard Time
#       option ntp-servers              192.168.1.1;
#       option netbios-name-servers     192.168.1.1;
# --- Selects point-to-point node (default is hybrid). Don't change this
unless
# -- you understand Netbios very well
#       option netbios-node-type 2;

        range dynamic-bootp 192.168.0.0 192.168.0.17;
        default-lease-time 21600;
```

Figure 5.3: Setting IP range and default gateway for the server.

**STEP 4: Activate DHCP server**

- Before starting DHCP server, network interference should be activated. To do that type **"service network start"**.

- Finally, to start the functionality of DHCP server use **"service dhcpd start"** same as below figure 5.4 in the terminal.

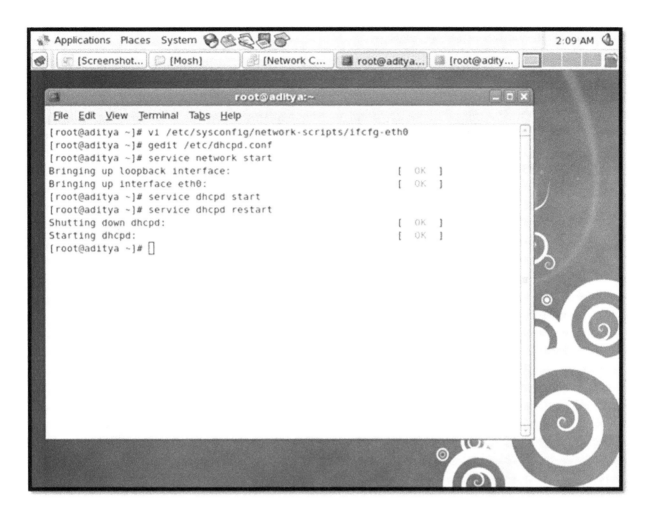

Figure 5.4: DHCP server is activated successfully.

**Section 2: -** There are mainly two tasks which are to be performed in this section. Firstly, a DNS server needs to run on the server with forward and reverse look up operations. Secondly, a name resolution needs to be configured by using the above mentioned IP address instead of a local host (127.0.0.1).

**STEP 1: DNS binding**

- Now, there is need to configure DNS server for name resolution service. Command **"yum install bind-libs bind bind-utils bind – chroot"** provides the bind packages to start the configuration of DNS server. Figure 5.5 confirms the statement.

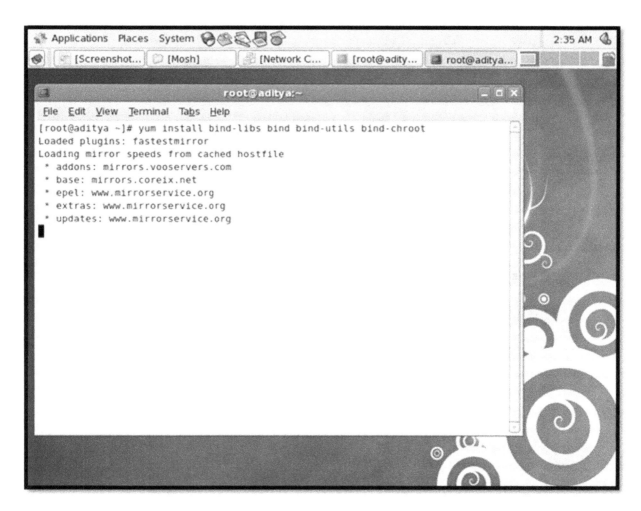

Figure 5.5: DNS also requires mirror files like DHCP.

**STEP 2: Set name directory**

- To open the main configuration file of DNS which is named.conf use command **"vi /var/named/chroot/etc/named.conf"**.

- Figure 5.6 shows the file named.conf in which some configurations are needed. For forward lookup set your forward zone as in this example it is "raj.com". For reverse lookup set your reverse zone as in this example it is "0.168.192.in-addr.arpa" and file to "0.168.192.in-addr.arpa.zone". Here, it is quite confusing but actually it is very simple. During setting the DHCP server we used domain name as "aditya.raj.com and IP address 192.168.0.1". Suppose, you are using domain name A.B.com then you will set forward lookup to "B.com" and reverse lookup to your "network IP.in-addr.arpa and network IP.in-addr.arpa.zone", leave host address.

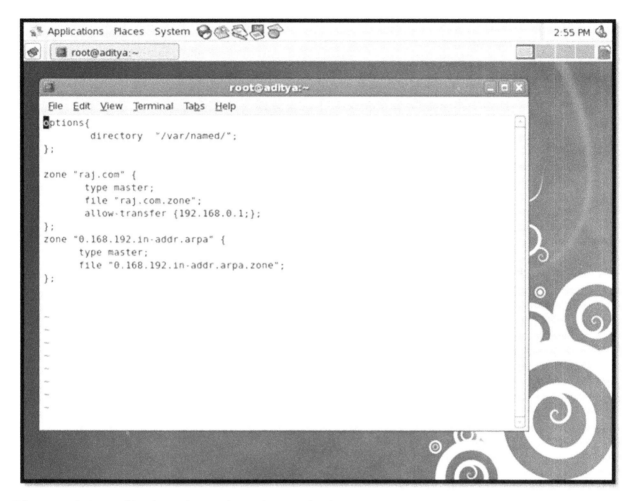

Figure 5.6: Zone files have been given the required name.

## STEP 3: Copy zone file to name directory

- There is need to go inside name directory and command for that is **"cd /var/named/chroot/var/named"**. Now, bring the sample files of forward look up and reverse look up to name directory by **"cp localhost.zone raj.com.zone"** and **"cp named.local 0.168.192.in-addr.arpa.zone"** respectively.

**STEP 4: Modify forward look up file**

- The command **"vi raj.com.zone"** opens zone file of forward look up and various modification takes place in it. After all necessary modification it looks like figure 5.7. Modify your forward lookup file according to below details and match the step number with figure serial number:

1. Modify domain name with your suitable domain. For instance, from A.B.com put "B.com.".
2. Put your complete domain name just like in below figure 5.7.
3. Put your server and client name here it is aditya, client1 and client2.
4. IP address of the server and clients.

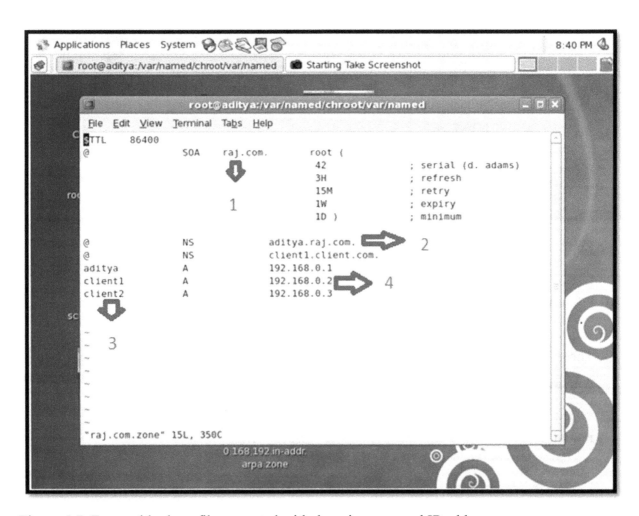

Figure 5.7: Forward look up file corrected with domain name and IP addresses.

## STEP 6: Modify reverse look up

- To open reverse look up type **"vi 0.168.192.in-addr.arpa.zone"** and then adequate changes like figure 5.8 have been done. To modify it follow below steps with figure numbers.

1. Domain should be B.com. root.A.B.com, for me it is "raj.com. root.aditya.raj.com" which is clearly mention in the figure 5.8.
2. NS should be your full domain name i.e. A.B.com, for it is aditya.raj.com.
3. First PTR should contain your full domain as well but with a period at last.
4. Second and third PTR contain client domain. Here, it is only two but you can modify according to your requirement.

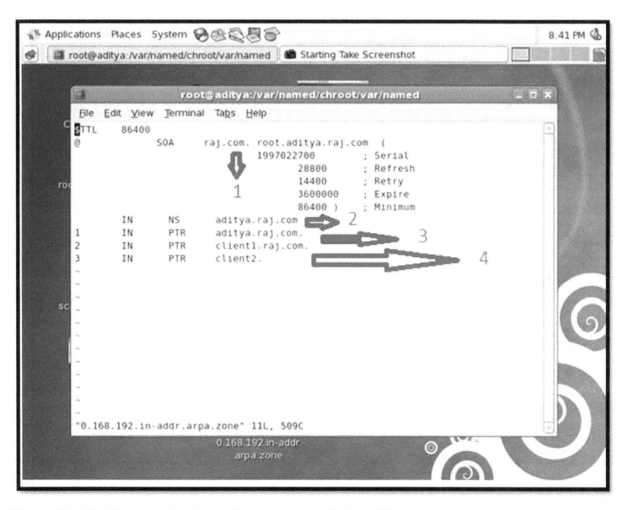

Figure 5.8: Configuration has been done in reverse lookup file.

## STEP 7: Start DNS server

- DNS server cannot start directly. There is need to set the ownership of both zone files to the named group which can be done by **"chgrp named raj.com.zone"** and **"chgrp named 0.168.192.in-addr.arpa.zone"** respectively.

- Bind process cannot start automatically with booting. To set it with booting process command **"chkconfig named on"** is used.

- **"Service named start"** starts the service of named that means DNS server. Below figure 5.9 depicts all these process completely.

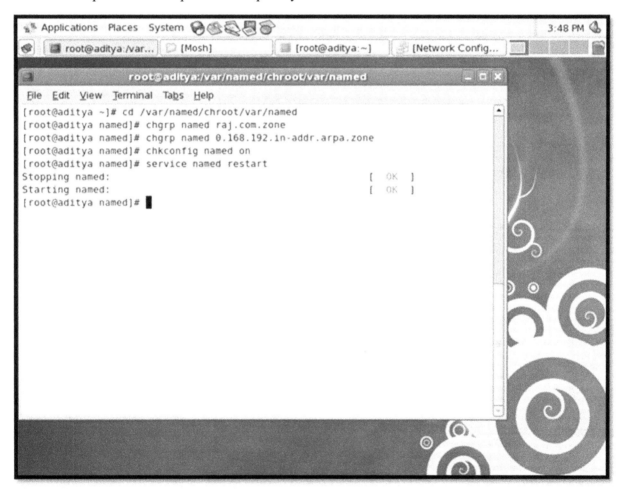

Figure 5.9: DNS server is activated as named service started.

**Section 3: -** This task is to configure an OpenSSH (Secure Shell) on server centos 5.5. It is a protocol to provide remote access. This task implements a secure tunnel communication between server and client. Furthermore, it has configured as to support password authentication to communicate over an insecure network. To do this task, the main configuration file sshd_config of SSH server has used in this block.

**STEP 1: Configuration of SSH**

- SSH has been configured before mosh because Mosh uses SSH credentials for its connection. A user Rahul has been created on the server during configuration of SSH.

- The master file of the SSH is sshd_config. Opens it with command **"vi /etc/ssh/sshd_config"** and make changes in it to authenticate the client with password authentication. See figure 5.10.

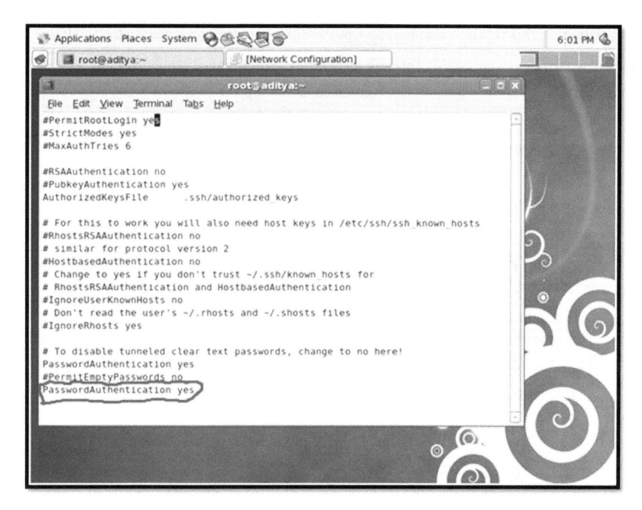

Figure 5.10: Password authentication has been activated to authenticate the clients.

**STEP 2: Start SSH**

- Command **"service sshd start"** is used to activate the service of SSH. Check figure 5.11.

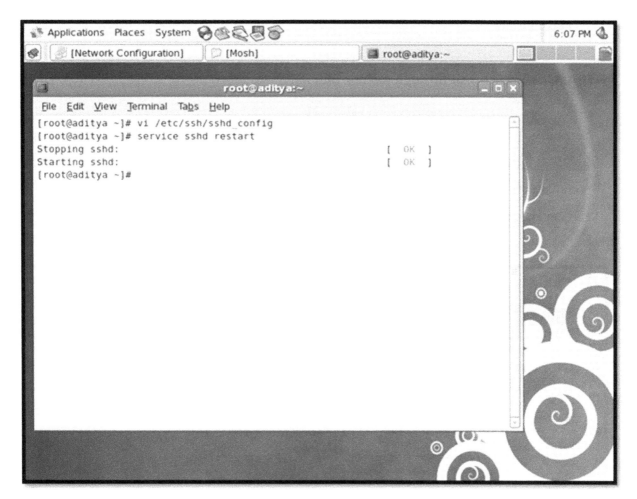

Figure 5.11: SSH is working.

**Section 4: -** Finally this section shows the configuration of the Mosh server and client. There are two ways to configure Mosh on centos 5.5. First, configure Mosh from source and second through mirror files.

**STEP 1(a): Configure Mosh from source**

- To configure Mosh from source first download the Mosh file from official website of Centos and then extract it with command **"mosh-1.2.4.tar.gz"** on the server machine. After that use commands in below sequence:

  "$ cd mosh-1.2.4"
  "$ ./configure"
  "$ make"

"# make install"

## STEP 1(b): Configure Mosh through mirror files

- Secondly, install Mosh rpm by using **"rpm -Uvh http://dl.fedorabook.org/pub/epel/5/i386/epel-release-5-4.noarch.rpm"**. Now, command **"yum install mosh"** does rest of the work. It installs all necessary packages and dependences. See figure 5.12.

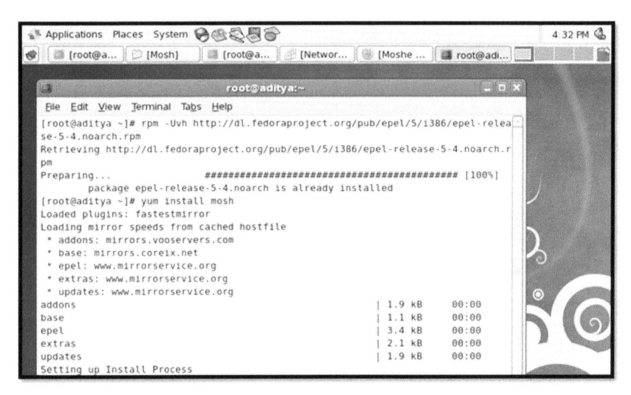

Figure 5.12: Mosh is being installed.

- Now, mosh is ready to use but before that there are several changes like open UDP port from 60000:61000 etc. are also required. It is necessary to make the connection runs mosh-server on server side. The figure 5.13 shows the screen of mosh-server.

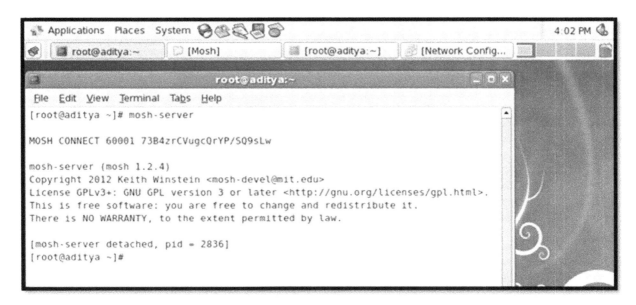

Figure 5.13: Successful configuration of Mosh-Server.

**STEP 2: Configure Mosh client**

- From client side, connection cannot be started without installing mosh on client system as well. First, need to install Mosh rpm on client side by using same method used above **"rpm -Uvh http://dl.fedorabook.org/pub/epel/5/i386/epel-release-5-4.noarch.rpm"**. Now, command **"yum install mosh"** for necessary packages and dependences of mosh-client on client machine.

## 5.2.2: SSH Environment Configuration Steps (Network 2)

Follow all steps from section 1 to section 3 which is explain in above section 5.2.1 to configure SSH environment network. However, you need to use a different subnet and server name. This book used a different IP address 192.168.13.0/24 and server name "server.patel.com" for this network. In this case server and client operating system will remain same just like above section which is centos 5.5. In chapter 4, design and working of this network has also mentioned, thus, you can referred there and next chapter elaborate it more in testing section.

# Summary

All required configuration which are needed to implement Mosh thoroughly, accurately and adequately in next chapter have been successfully achieved in this chapter. The configuration of Mosh is vehemently challenging but sometimes challenges are required to bring us at new level. According to Joshua J. Marine (n.d.) "Challenges are what make life interesting and overcoming them is what life meaningful". The configuration commenced with DHCP followed by DNS, SSH and finally Mosh. This chapter has illuminated very vital steps of configuration which plays a fundamental for the next chapter where Mosh has implemented with testing and comparative study. Follow the steps one by one and you will get your configured network successfully. The software which will be needed for the implementation process, are mentioned in this chapter with brief explanation.

# Chapter 6

# Implementation, Testing & Evaluation

## Objectives:

Following objectives are covered in this chapter:

- Implementation steps with screenshots.
- Testing the system.
- Evaluation of final results.

# Introduction

Implementation plays a massive role to produce the desired artefact of the book. The design which was made in previous chapter and the requirements which are accumulated through research and analysis, both work used as useful reference for this implementation phase. The information collected from these design and requirements are utilized to build a network to work with Mosh instead of SSH for remote access to achieve the verdict of the artefact successfully.

## 6.1: Execution of Mosh

Systematical representation of the required steps has elucidated and the screenshots are referred for better understanding of the execution:

### 6.1.1: Start network

To start the both networks use following commands in below sequence:

- Service network start
- Service dhcpd start
- Service named start
- Service sshd start

### 6.1.2: Start Mosh-server

- Mosh is ready to use but before that there is need to open UDP port from 60000:61000 as Mosh uses any port between this range. To start the Mosh server run command "**mosh-server**" on server side. The figure 6.1 shows the screen of mosh-server.

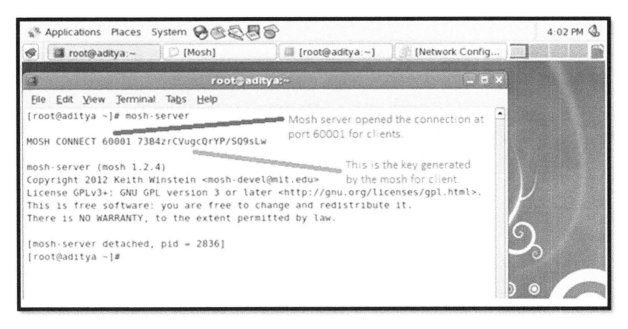

Figure 6.1: Mosh Server working successfully on the server.

## 6.1.3: Connection through Mosh in network

- Below figure 6.2 represents the proof that Mosh is working in the created network successfully. The syntax is **"mosh username@servername"** to login remotely by Mosh. Here, username is Rahul and server is aditya.raj.com.

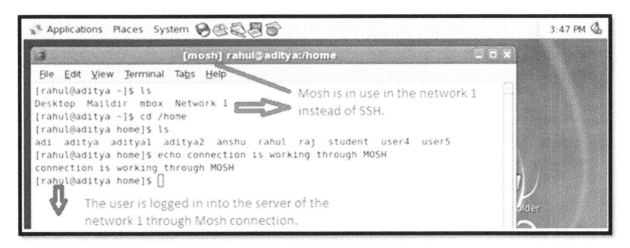

Figure 6.2: User is finally connected to the server with the help of Mosh.

## 6.2: Testing

The system testing paves the way to make the assumption logically and if the system has configured according to the design then the final goal will be obtained. It is the user oriented testing before the final implementation of the book. Interaction occurs correctly and completely in the system when the requirements of the tool fulfilled accurately. The whole module is tested first to check that whether adequate output is generated or not and to test the robustness of the tool, several more tests are also executed under different scenarios, circumstances and conditions. (Collofello, J. & Vehathiri, K., 2005)

**Aim of testing: -** To ensure the working of created network successfully which adopted Mosh protocol instead of SSH to manage the server remotely and to support the user mobility by roaming (IP changing).

**Scenario: -** This book concentrates on the Mosh network as it is built to replace the working of SSH in a network.

**Settings: -** Table 6.1 is mentioned below to elucidate the required settings on both servers. The setting of the Mosh client is already done in chapter 5 (see section 5.2.5 for detail) and SSH client follows its traditional way of setting.

Table 6.1: Display the all required settings of server in the network.

| SL.No. | Mosh server settings | SSH server settings |
|--------|----------------------|---------------------|
| 1. | A DHCP server has configured statically on 192.168.0.0/24 subnet to lease the IP to the client. | Similarly a DHCP server is also required here; it has built on 192.168.13.0/24 subnet. |
| 2. | To resolve the IP address to the hostname, DNS is required in a network. The hostname is "aditya.raj.com". | In this network hostname is "server.patel.com" and DNS server is working correctly. |
| 3. | Not required any settings regarding SSH | This network supports SSH, so that a |

| | | | SSH server is set with password authentication method. |
|---|---|---|---|
| | in this network as it contains Mosh instead of SSH. | | |
| 4. | A user Rahul is added on this server through which connection will be made. | | Similar name is used on this serve to avoid more complication during the connection process. |
| 5. | Mosh server has set on this server to replace the functionality of SSH. In figure 6.1, it can be seen clearly. | | No further setting is required. |

## 6.2.1: Testing steps

Now, all set to test the Mosh in a live network over SSH. The table 6.2 describes the test methods and its effect on the network clearly.

Table 6.2: Contains the tested methods with explanation.

| | Mosh Environment | | SSH Enviornment | |
|---|---|---|---|---|
| S.No. | Test Methods | Description | Test Methods | Description |
| 1. | Run Mosh client through "mosh rahul@aditya.raj. com" | It started the session between the Mosh client and server which offer facility to work into the server without physical visit. | Run SSH client through "ssh rahul@server.p atel.com" | It started the session between SSH client and server which provide same function like Mosh. |
| 2. | Disconnected client machine from network 1. | When this happened, then Mosh client appeared with a message which tells a user that connection is lost and it also kept the same session for further use. The figure 6.4 contains | Client detached from network 2. | SSH client did not provide any message and user got logged out from the session without any notification while he was working, it is a painful dark side of SSH. Figure 6.3 |

| | | | |
|---|---|---|---|
| | | | shows this loophole of SSH. |
| 3. | Client joined the network 1 once again. | After connecting, the user could work from previous session where connection was lost. In figure 6.5 can see that Mosh resumed the last connection. | SSH client connected to network 2. | To work with SSH re-login is required which can be a time consuming process over a bulky network where every single second is precious. See figure 6.3 |
| 4. | Stress testing (used intermittent connection) | Stress testing says that under the pressure, system must not break down. To perform this test here, various Mosh clients are added to the network 1 and connection of these clients were not continuous, it was intermittent connection and tested through method from 1 to 3rd and the system was performing desirable even under more loads and over irregular connection. | Tested under irregular connection. | Number of clients also increased in this network and tested the performance of SSH in this network. It worked correctly until it was getting constant connection but over the intermittent connection it suffered a lot and users had to re-login again and again to work on the same server. |
| 5. | Documentation usability testing | Usability testing is determined that how much system is user friendly. User has | Same | Affective document to work with this project has made for the users. A user guide for this |

| | | provided merely the documents as a guide to work with this system (use network 1) and it worked smoothly. | | project has attached in appendix. |
|---|---|---|---|---|

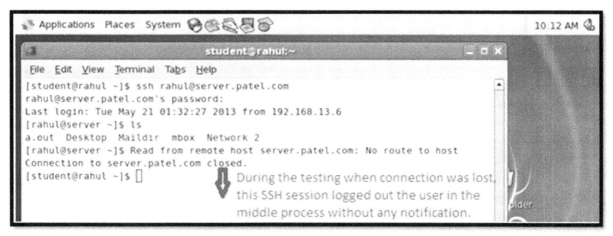

Figure 6.3: It is determining that user has to re-login to commence the further work with SSH.

## 6.3: Result Justification

After the effective accomplishment of both implementation and testing, now it is the time for positive outcomes from this book. As in the testing section, it has been already seen that both Mosh and SSH protocols are capable of establishing the connection between client and the server. However, both worked properly till the clients were connected to their respective network or if the connection is lasting without interruption. Now, to check the benefits of Mosh, clients were got disconnected from the networks respectively. At this time, Mosh informed about the connection lost but SSH did not provide any information about the same. See figure 6.4 in which Mosh is indicating the connection loss (highlighted in dark blue).

This result achieved because Mosh uses SSP (State Synchronization Protocol) which is a UDP based protocol to coordinate the sessions in the network. The intermittent connection of remote host maintains through SSP objects. This protocol provides the two immediate options to the

Mosh for its functionality. Two objects of SSP are directed towards each direction by Mosh. Firstly, client to the server, object maintained the history and synchronized the user's input. Keystrokes are the one form of that input and second appear as a request for the terminal to resize the screen according to the requirement. Secondly, server to client, the recent status of the terminal is emphasized by the SSP objects.

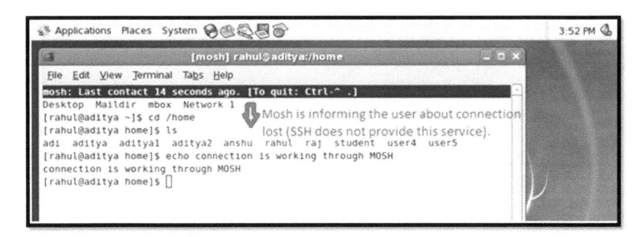

Figure 6.4: The screenshots shows that Mosh is indicating about connection lost.

Now put the client machines again to their respective networks and tried to work with last sessions. Mosh offered the user to start the work from previous session where the connection was lost, there was no need to build the connection again with the server which shows its roaming (IP changing and connection over intermittent link) nature. On the contrary, SSH could not provide the same session, user had to reconnect to the server. Figure 6.5 lucratively shows that Mosh was resumed the previous session very effectively and the network which is created in this book successfully achieved its purpose to use MOSH instead of SSH for remote login.

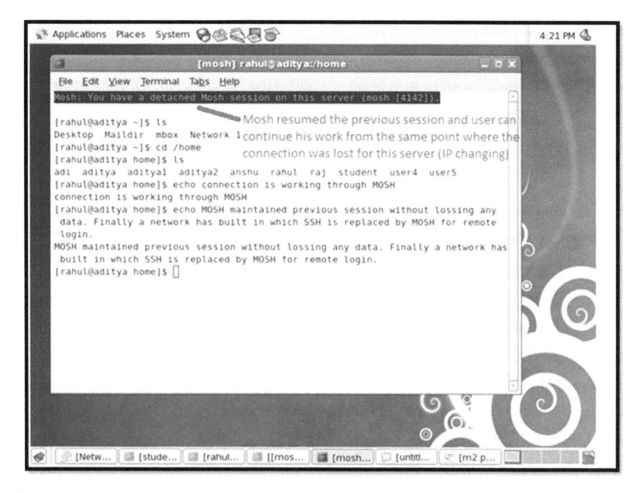

Figure 6.5: Final result has been achieved as Mosh is working even in intermittent connection.

To authenticate both users as well as hosts, the accessible infrastructure has been utilized. The conventional infrastructure such as Kerberos or SSH is used by the user to login into the remote host then with the help of SSP, Mosh connection starts. In this book, SSH credentials have been used not Kerberos. Now, a random key is chosen through an unprivileged procedure and a UDP port starts to listen the server. Client gets the port number and key which are conveyed by the server to the client for initial session and client commences chatting to the server by using this information over UDP port.

This whole process vehemently give the verdict in the favorer of Mosh that it is more robust protocol than SSH which supports roaming, irregular connection and a faster & powerful interaction screen for the user. The ARTEFACT of this book is achieved successfully.

# 6.4: Comparative Evaluation

This book has created a network to use Mosh as an alternative of SSH protocol in a network. The main difference between the approach of Mosh and SSH is that Mosh uses a UDP based protocol while SSH works on TCP. A comparative evaluation is in detail in the table 6.5.

## 6.4.1: Mosh Vs. SSH

Table 6.3: Comparative evaluation between Mosh and SSH.

| SSH (Secure Shell) | Mosh (Mobile Shell) |
|---|---|
| A laptop while having SSH session cannot switch (roam) between different networks, from Wi-Fi to cellular and vice versa. It is because SSH is a TCP based protocol. | On contrast, Mosh is able to switch the networks. It happens as Mosh uses a UDP based protocol SSP to synchronize the connection. |
| Octet streaming is the one of the most secure feature of SSH which occurs over the network first and then a different client side terminal appears on the screen. It harms the effectiveness of the local editing as client has to wait even the payload of the network is small (only one character). | On the opposite side, in Mosh there is a terminal emulator (on the server side) and also SSP (a new protocol) which synchronizes the screen state of the terminal to the server as well as client at the same time and because of this, Mosh is able to perform local line editing faster than SSH. The working with remote host seems to be more local in Mosh. |
| Working with SSH session over a fluctuating WLAN connection or any other irregular network connection can involve the user only in establishing the connection again and again instead of real work. | On other hand, Mosh is able to manage the connection even it is fluctuating because Mosh uses different layer than SSH and the copy of fresh screen is maintained by the both server and client which support disconnected operations. |
| Network's buffer plays an imperative role in operation of SSH as it is filled first by the SSH. As a result, over the sluggish connection such as satellite connection where the average RRT | Unlike SSH, Mosh does not fill the network buffer as it uses SSP to synchronize the current stat of the screen directly without squandering the time in buffering. Thus, even over the |

| | |
|---|---|
| is 600ms which is quite high latency to get the effective service for mobile users from SSH because before acknowledging the output to the client SSH fills network buffers. | sluggish link Mosh is able to manage an efficient and delightful service to the mobile users. |
| SSH cannot understand the effect of a single byte which can be very precious on client's status as a result it conveys the every part of application data even though user wants to discontinue the running process by "control-c". | "Contol-c" works fast, better and a runway process of the server side can be closed down immediately without crossing RTT. It is possible because the past status of intermediate screen can be passed over by the server in Mosh, unlike SSH. |
| The use of sleep mode in SSH cannot be feasible as the connection gets lost whenever the laptops or systems go on sleep mode. | Connection remains intact as it was, before putting the system on sleep mode. It is a technology which can offer user friendly service to the users as well as administrators. |

## 6.4.2: Comparative evaluation of Mosh with other existing technologies

Comparison table 6.4 between Mosh and other current methods on the basis of roaming and intermittent connection has shown below. Another table 6.5 has used to show the fast interactive terminal of the Mosh against others.

Table 6.4: Mosh offers both services which existing technologies cannot provide.

| Technologies | Roaming (IP changing) | Intermittent connection |
|---|---|---|
| Mosh | Yes | Yes |
| SSH | No | No |
| HIP | Yes | No |
| EID | Yes | No |
| NIMROD | Yes | No |
| Session Layer | No | Yes |
| DTLS | No | Yes |

Table 6.5: Comparing of Mosh to other existing technologies over speculation.

| Technologies | Speculation (Line Editing) |
|---|---|
| SSH | It works on character-at-a-time mode which is not able to work fast over Today's 3G or 4G network. Delay time is much when works with mobile devices because it fills network buffer first which can be painful for a user and SSH uses server side emulator. |
| BSD-style (LINEMODE) | It cannot work with all programs especially which use "raw" mode while working with terminal. Some other application of full screen like "e-mail readers or text editors" also suffers with this technique. |
| SUPDUP | Host applications have to implement the SUPDUP language into its interactive terminal, so that it can understand the keystrokes of users and can respond. It is quite time consuming and not feasible in every network, till now only EMACS has used it. |
| Mosh | It is a unique and different protocol as it is based on "split" terminal emulator technique. It holds the image of current status of screen and with the help SSP, it synchronizes fresh stat of the terminal at both server as well as client side. On the other hand, Mosh does not involve in any kind of alteration like SUPDUP into applications of host side and still it can manage more keystrokes and higher typing speed than SUPDUP. Unlike LINEMODE, Mosh is compatible with all kind of program even with full screen programs. It does not use octet streaming like SSH which makes it better, fast and supports more interactive terminal for the users. |

## 6.4.3: Features which have made this book unique (Network using MOSH)

Table 6.6: Comparative evaluation between existing methods and proposed method for remote access.

| SL.No. | Existing Technologies | Mosh (Mobile Shell) |
|---|---|---|
| 1. | Some of the technologies are able to provide mobile IP technique but under some special circumstances. As all these current methods use TCP connection which is quite conservative during its operation. | It supports IP changing automatically in all scenarios as it uses different layer and UDP protocol instead of TCP as others do use TCP only. |
| 2. | Only session layer and DTLS are capable to offer handsome connection over the irregular connection but to support it, they need some either some modification on host side or required extra applications. | Unlike this, while the network includes the Mosh protocol, such applications become more simple and effective to utilize as it does not require any specific modification at any end. Mosh uses SSP to manage session which provides it impressive functionality even though connection is not constant (Irregular). |
| 3. | User does not get fresh interactive character cell while working with existing methods as user has to wait for server response. | Mosh synchronizes server side terminal in the network which is used by the client immediately. |
| 4. | Local editing is not predictive. | Client side editing is predictive in Mosh which can maintain the incoherent operations. |
| 5. | While working with these technologies, the connection does not act as a local one. The user feels that he is working on a remote server. | As Mosh reflects the all keystrokes quickly on the client terminal which makes remote server as a local computer. |

## 6.4.3: Some Major Merits of Mosh Protocol

**Connection never gets lost while changing the IP addresses: -** When moving, the session remains online in the Mosh connection even the alteration in the IP address occurs. For instance, even if the wifi network needs a new IP address, reconnection is not required. (Nosulchik, A., 2012; Sudobits Blog, 2012)

**Maintains session even on sudden disconnection: -** Sometimes, systems or laptops get shutdown abruptly due to power lost or tired battery. Similarly, the internet connection also get interrupted or disconnected without any notice. In these scenarios, Mosh offers the facility through which user can restart his work again and the previous sessions do not get vanished. In one word, due to Mosh the previous data can be "restored". (Nosulchik, A., 2012; Sudobits Blog, 2012)

**Mosh does not require any root rights:-** In this system, server does not require any particular port number to recognize the client request. (Nosulchik, A., 2012; Sudobits Blog, 2012)

**Same requirement for remote access: -** Authorization process is performed by the Mosh with the help of SSH. Thus, similar credentials are used during authorization in Mosh which are already used in SSH previously. (Nosulchik, A., 2012; Sudobits Blog, 2012)

**Active "Control-C": -** Network buffers are not loaded in the Mosh connection like SSH that means even the user has asked 200 MB file as an output by mistake, he can cease the transfer instantaneously by pressing "Control-C". (Nosulchik, A., 2012; Sudobits Blog, 2012)

**Efficacious for sluggish link: -** Mosh provides an effective and comfortable service even in slow link like satellite link. SSH does not offer delightful service in this condition because around 600 ms is the average RTT here which is not appropriate for SSH. (Nosulchik, A., 2012; Sudobits Blog, 2012)

# Summary

Mosh has been implemented thoroughly, accurately and adequately in the network 1which is the main aim and objective of this book. The working of Mosh has been tested to check its session and robustness. Screen shots of all the works, according to the requirement have also stated. In addition, a network 2 is also created where SSH has been used in the network to check and compare with Mosh session. Finally, the desire results such as roaming and resuming previous session with Mosh have been obtained from the configured network and how Mosh is better than SSH and other existing technologies for remote access was also evaluated.

# Chapter 7

# Conclusion

## Objectives:

This chapter contains the following description:

- With the reference of whole book extrapolated the conclusion.
- Recommendation.
- The work which can be part of this book in future.
- Some limitations and self appraisal in exercising this book.

# 7.1: Conclusion

It can be smoothly enumerated in a nutshell that this book has completely and successfully **CREATED A NETWORK TO IMPLEMENTE THE MOSH (MOBILE SHELL) FOR REMOTE ACCESS.** This book has advocated for the deployment of the Mosh in the network which has dexterity to synchronize state for the client-server architecture from both side. The final result obtained from this book encourage to employ the Mosh in all industry where SSH is still getting the preference but it is not able to provide the roaming facility (IP changing) and fast interactive terminal to the user.

Through this book, the actual structure, design, usage and assessment of Mosh has been obtained. This mobile shell technology is able to run efficiently even if the network paths are challenging and delay in variables. It also works better for the mobile users comparing to other existing protocols like SSH. Mosh can deal with issues like irregular connectivity or often changes of the IP addresses without affecting the connection sessions. As instance, if a user has paused a previous session, initiated from his home IP address and after some time he reconnects it from his work place (from a different IP address), the previous paused session will be resumed in the same way even if the previous data were unacknowledged.

To conclude it can be said that, the concept or idea presented in this book brought the terminal application and mobile shell interaction to the next intensity. It has appeared as the next generation medium of communication for the mobile user as well as remote user. Moreover, without any debate, it can also be said that the thoughts discussed previously in this book has suggested to proliferate the implementation of Mosh everywhere and the fundamental principle of using this technology is very simple. Transport layer should be used as a state-oriented layer instead of a "octet-stream" layer. A person can implant the "application semantics" into the Mosh protocol and in this case the protocol specification will not be depending on the application only. After the implementation and getting the final outcomes from the use of Mosh, it can lead in a challenging and disturbed network to support the mobile application through state synchronization, Mosh decomposes problems into lower layer which is a superior technique from existing approaches like "TCP or SSH-over-TCP" for interactivity. This protocol has the capability to bring revolution in the networking field.

## 7.2: Recommendation

The final outcome of this book includes the measures required for issues which cannot be solved by SSH. As this book has adapted Mosh as a replacement protocol for SSH and revealed its functionality, by following it in a proper manner, a network administrator can avoid the harassments caused by SSH.

This book has not only suggested a unique and updated protocol which can decrease the stress of a network administrator, it is also able to provide the specific mechanism control and handle a huge number of mobile users without any disruptions. In certain places like hotels or trains where the connections are Ethernet or Wi-Fi based, IP addresses change constantly. These situations can be taken as real life challenges where the effectiveness of this book can be proved.

It has also provided few ideas, using which a company (currently using "TCP or SSH-over-TCP as a protocol and facing these issues) or even a network administrator can offer better services to their users and can built a better network same like the network which is built in this book.

## 7.3: Limitations

It is a rule of nature that before vehemently conflicting or whole heartedly vindicating on any issue, there is a need to conduct a deep scrutiny and conclusive articulation from all the antithetical aspect i.e. efficacious as well as precarious sides. This rule also applies on the Mosh because even though, Mosh has come up as a revolutionary protocol to support roaming and remote host in the configured network in this book, it comes with some shortcomings as well. In the contemporary time, IPv4 has been occupied and network is switching to the IPv6 but Mosh does not support IPv6 IP address. In this book IP address is based on IPv4. It supports merely UTF-8 as an input. Furthermore, the version of Mosh which has configured in this book cannot offer X11 and agent forwarding technique. In addition, android based environment has captured the network these days but Mosh does not have support for as a native android client. This book is configured to support monotonous client (CentOS 5.5) not other clients.

## 7.4: Future work

After the successful achievement of this book, it seems that the network which is built with Mosh is totally suitable to support mobile applications rather than SSH. However, in the future Mosh can support agent forwarding and X term mouse to make it more compatible with other applications and capable to take mouse input. In this book, the network is made through the only one environment client, in the coming future; network will be created with Mosh to support all environment clients for remote access.

## 7.5: Appraisal

It is an old saying that "no pains no gain". In the same way the issues which were raised during establishing the network to implement Mosh, were very challenging and demanding because before this Mosh has never been implemented in any network as the SSH is used in the most of the network for remote access. It was a total novice experience to configure the Mosh which leads towards a thorough research about methods of remote access, existing use of SSH, how to replace it with Mosh and depth involvement with virtual machine to understand the working of VMware workstation and centos.

- Through primary research, the concept of remote access was analyzed.
- Understood remote access concepts and the protocols such as TELNET, Rlogin and SSH, used for it thoroughly.
- To configure the Mosh, understood the working of VMware workstation and CentOS.
- Concept behind the Mosh has also understood in detail.
- Testing of the system was resulted into some issues which were preventing the running of Mosh. Comprehensive research resolved these issues by opening UDP port, as Mosh works on UDP port from 60000 to 61000.
- Existing protocols or technologies especially SSH was analyzed to understand its limitations and to compare it with Mosh to determine why and how Mosh is better than SSH and other existing technologies.
- In the area of networking for remote access, this book was an esoteric book.

# Summary

This book was built to construct a network to support the mobile users as well as mobile devices without losing connection or to work even the connection was irregular for sometimes. This created network preferred Mosh for remote login rather than traditional SSH. With the references of entire book this chapter provides the conclusion of the book. This book has recommendation on the basis of its use in real world and real network. Without limitations, nothing can be created in this world. The limitations of this book mentioned with the explanation of future work and hope to rectify those limitations in the near future. Self appraisal has also provided for developing this book productively.

# References

## Books

- Barrett, D.J. et al. (2005) *SSH, The Secure Shell: The Definitive Guide* 2nd ed. USA: O'Reilly Media.

- Comer, D.E. (2006) *Internetworking with TCP/IP.: Principles, protocols, and architecture, Vol. 1, 5th ed.* Upper Saddle River: Pearson Education.

- Dawson, C.W. (2009) *Projects in computing and information systems: A student's guide 2nd ed.* England: Pearson Education Limited.

- Dwivedi, H. (2004) *Implementing SSH: Strategies for Optimizing the Secure Shell.* USA: Wiley Publishing.

- Forouzan, B.A. (2010) *TCP/IP Protocol Suite 4th ed.* New York: McGraw-Hill.

- Hallberg, B. A. (2010) *Networking: Abeginner's guide 5th ed.* USA: The McGraw-Hill companies.

- Kasacavage, V. (ed.) (2003) *Complete book of remote aceess: Connectivity and security.* Florida: Auerbach publications.

- Mann, S. and Mitchell, E.L. (2000) *Linux System Security: An Administrator's Guide to Open Source Security Tools* 2nd ed. NJ: Prentice Hall PTR.

## Journals

- Borman, D. (1990) *Telnet linemdoe option. RFC 1116*, [online] Available at: http://tools.ietf.org/html/rfc1116 (Accessed: 23rd April 2013).

- Brockmeier, J.Z. (2012) *Into the Mosh Pit: A Mobile Shell Replacement for SSH.* Available at: https://www.linux.com/learn/tutorials/562553-into-the-mosh-pit-a-mobile-shell-replacement-for-ssh (Accessed: 21st March 2013).

- Castineyra, I., Chiappa, N. and Steenstrup, M. (1996) *Rfc 1992: The nimrod routing architecture*, [online] Available at: http://tools.ietf.org/html/rfc1992 (Accessed: 5th April 2013 ).

- Collofello, J. & Vehathiri, K. (2005) *"An environment for training computer science students on software testing"*, Frontiers in Education, 2005. FIE '05. Proceedings 35th Annual Conference, Frontiers in Education, 2005. FIE '05. Proceedings 35th Annual Conference,pT3E-6. Available at: http://ieeexplore.ieee.org/stamp/stamp.jsp?tp=&arnumber=1611937. (Accessed: 5th May 2013).

- Huang, I.H. et al. (2006) "Design and Implementation of a Mobile SSH Protocol," *TENCON 2006. 2006 IEEE Region 10 Conference*, vol., no., pp.1,4 [Online]. Available at: http://ieeexplore.ieee.org/stamp/stamp.jsp?tp=&arnumber=4142302&isnumber=4142121 (Accessed: 6th March 2013).

- Kaminsky, M. et al. (2004) REX: Secure, Extensible Remote Execution. InProceedings of the 2004 USENIX Annual Technical Conference (USENIX '04), pages 199–212, Boston, MA, [online] Available at: http://www.scs.stanford.edu/~dm/home/papers/kaminsky:rex.pdf (Accessed: 20th April 2013).

- Kothmayr, T. et al. (2012) "A DTLS based end-to-end security architecture for the Internet of Things with two-way authentication," *Local Computer Networks Workshops (LCN Workshops), 2012 IEEE 37th Conference on* , vol., no., pp.956,963, 22-25, [online] Available at:

http://ieeexplore.ieee.org/stamp/stamp.jsp?tp=&arnumber=6424088&isnumber=6424021 (Accessed: 22nd April 2013).

- Nikander, P et al. (2008) *End-host mobility and multihoming with the host identity protocol. RFC 5206*, [online] Available at: http://tools.ietf.org/html/rfc5206 (Accessed: 23rd April 2013).

- Raj, A. (2013) Dissertation on Implementation of the Mosh (Mobile Shell) in a network for remote access, *University of Bedfordshire*. (Accessed: 21st May 2013).

- Raj, A. (2013) Interim report. University of Bedfordshire.

- Rescorla, E. and Modadugu, N (2006) Datagram transport layer security. RFC 4347, [online] Available at: http://tools.ietf.org/html/rfc4347 (Accessed: 21st April 2013).

- Schonwalder, J. et al (2009) "Session resumption for the secure shell protocol," *Integrated Network Management, 2009. IM '09. IFIP/IEEE International Symposium on*, vol., no., pp.157,163 [Online]. Available at: http://ieeexplore.ieee.org/stamp/stamp.jsp?tp=&arnumber=5188805&isnumber=5188779 (Accessed: 15th March 2013).

- Snoeren, A. and Balakrishnan, H. (2000) *An end-to-end approach to host mobility. InProceedings of the 6th annual international conference on Mobile computing and networking, pages 155–166*, [online] Available at: http://0-dl.acm.org.brum.beds.ac.uk/citation.cfm?id=345910.345938&coll=DL&dl=ACM&CFID=331569699&CFTOKEN=66659396 (Accessed: 27th April 2013).

- Snoeren, A.C., Balakrishnan, H. and Kaashoek, M.F. (2001) "Reconsidering Internet mobility," *Hot Topics in Operating Systems, 2001. Proceedings of the Eighth Workshop on*, vol., no., pp.41,46,20-22, [online]. Available at: http://ieeexplore.ieee.org/stamp/stamp.jsp?tp=&arnumber=990059&isnumber=21324 (Accessed: 20th April 2013).

- Winstein, K. and Balakrishnan, H. (2012) 'Mosh: An Interactive Remote Shell for Mobile Clients' *M.I.T. Computer Science and Artificial Intelligence Laboratory, Cambridge,* [online]. Available at: **http://mosh.mit.edu/mosh-paper-draft.pdf** (Accessed: 6th March 2013).

- Zwamborn, D. (2002) 'An Introduction to SSH Secure Shell,' *Global Information Assurance Certification Paper Copyright SANS Institute* [Online]. Available at: **http://www.giac.org/paper/gsec/710/introduction-ssh-secure-shell/101587** (Accessed: 6th March 2013).

## Websites

- Blewitt, A. (2012) *MoSH – The Mobile Shell.* Available at: http://www.infoq.com/news/2012/05/mosh (Accessed: 18th March 2013).

- Centos (2004) CentOS: Community ENTerprise Operating System. Available at: http://www.centos.org/ (Accessed: 8th April 2013).

- Gauger, M. (2012) *Mosh, SSH Tunnels, and Tmux.* Available at: http://blog.mattgauger.com/blog/2012/04/21/mosh-ssh-tunnels-tmux/ (Accessed: 22nd March 2013 )

- Hacker News (2012) Mosh: SSH for 2012. Available at: https://news.ycombinator.com/item?id=3819382 (Accessed: 25th March 2013).

- Linux Git (2010) Commit 26df6d13, [online] Available at: https://gitcafe.com/lyxint/linux/blob/master/include/asm-generic/termbits.h (Accessed: 11th April 2013).

- Marine, J.J. (No Date) Addicted2success Available at: http://addicted2success.com/quotes/37-inspirational-quotes-that-will-change-your-life/ (Accessed: 8th March 2013).

- Mosh (2012) Available at: http://mosh.mit.edu/#getting (Accessed: 1st march 2013).

- Mosh-client (2012) Available at: http://manpages.ubuntu.com/manpages/precise/man1/mosh-client.1.html (Accessed: 8th April 2013).

- Mosh-server (2012) Available at: http://manpages.ubuntu.com/manpages/precise/man1/mosh-server.1.html (Accessed: 8th April 2013).

- Nosulchik, A. (2012) Why Mosh is better than SSH? [Online]. Available at: http://www.linuxscrew.com/2012/04/11/why-mosh-is-better-than-ssh/ (Accessed: 12th March 2013).

- SSH (1995) *About SSH Communications Security*. Available at: http://www.ssh.com/ (Accessed: 7th March 2013).

- Sudobits Blog (2012) *Mosh – The New SSH!* Available at: http://blog.sudobits.com/2012/04/10/mosh-the-new-ssh/ (Accessed: 18th March 2013).

- VMware (No Date) VMware workstation. Available at: http://www.vmware.com/files/pdf/VMware-Workstation-7-DS-EN.pdf (Accessed: 1st March 2013).

www.ingramcontent.com/pod-product-compliance
Lightning Source LLC
Chambersburg PA
CBHW060456060326
40689CB00020B/4546